# WOMEN BUSINESS GUIDE TO WINNING CONTRACTS

A detailed guide for pursuing contracts with the Federal Government, Corporations, Local Counties and Other Entities

Antionette Ball

The Adiva Group
Atlanta, GA

## Women Owned Business Guide to Winning Contracts ™

Copyright @ 2018

All rights reserved. No part of this book may be reproduced in any form or by any means, electronic or mechanical, including photocopying and recording, or by an information storage and retrieval systems without written permission of the publisher, except for the including of brief quotations in an article or review.

Copies of this book are available at special discounts for bulk purchases for classes or training purposes.

Published by Adiva Group
235 Peachtree St., Suite 400
Atlanta, GA
404-681-2497

ISBN: 978-0-9761722-4-6
Library of Congress Control Number: 2018903035
Name: Antoinette Ball, Author
Description: Second Edition, Atlanta, Ga
Subjects: Business. Entrepreneurship.

Printed in the United States

Note: The information presented in this book is for educational purposes and not guaranteed to produce any results for any parties. The results may vary from individual to individual and how you will utilize this information. It is sold with the intent of providing useful information and resources.

A special thank you to all the special people that have contributed to the printing of this book

Latasha Ball, the most creative person that I need, a daughter who brings sunshine when she walks in the door

Marionette Ball, a sister who show uncompromising support

Yolanda White, a loving Niece, a constant breath of fresh air

Clifton, business mentor and constant supporter

My professional network of dedicated and resilient women entrepreneurs

To my wonderful inner circle of women who continue to support and inspire me – I appreciate you all and let's keep winning together!

# INTRODUCTION

I have personally experienced the excitement, challenges and ups and downs of being an entrepreneur. Over the last two decades I have created programs, conducted hundreds of hours of business coaching to support the growth of women in business. I am also one of the founders of The Women's Entrepreneurial Opportunity Project, Inc., WEOP, an organization dedicated to the mission of supporting business development and growth that targets women owned and operated businesses.

The vision of this book was to share my knowledge and information with a growing segment of women trying to find success in the business world. Along my journey, I have met some amazing women willing to share information and resources that have been extremely helpful for my advancement.

This book is not just for women owned businesses; it can also be beneficial for Consultants, Freelancers, Contractors and women pursuing business ventures. The overall goal is to educate women about business and encourage them to be creative in their approach and take advantage of all beneficial programs and opportunities that support women in business.

Throughout this book, you will be introduced to strategies that will encourage you to think about how you can be strategic and leverage your status as a woman owned business.

This book is for you, especially if you fall into one of the following categories:

- You are currently a small business owner and seeking to enter the federal marketplace and want to learn how to navigate the process.

- You are operating a business and want to expand your business with contracts in the private sector, which includes counties, cities and governments.
- You are considering launching a business and want to learn how to secure contracts in the public and private sectors.
- You are a business consultant and you want to acquire skills to educate your customers about how to diversify their opportunities with contracts.
- You are a business owner and want to learn how to navigate government databases and develop strategies that can help you grow your business with contracts.
- You are a consultant or an independent contract and would eventually like to pursue a prime contract opportunity, however, you are interested in pursuing subcontracting opportunities.

There is no magic formula for achieving success in business, however, if you really take time to do your research, plan and be consistent and methodical in how you approach business, you can win. What will be your differentiator is to really take time and continue to make sure you understand the "why" with every business decision.

You can set yourself **ABOVE** the competition with the following formula:

**A**sk questions and do your research

**B**e strategic about how you posture yourself – leverage all your status

**O**pportunities are abundant and take steps to prepare

**V**enture forward and understand how to do research and know where to go to find the information

**E**xplore opportunities and understand the contracting language for the federal government and private sector

The underlying message that will resonate from this book is to continue to educate yourself, do your research, market your business, build your team and learn how you can leverage your women owned business status.

We hope that you will find this information valuable and useful in your journey as a business owner, entrepreneurs or when you are just doing business.

This book is filled jam packed with information, insightful, resources for you to build and work on your business. Sit back, relax, enjoy and **EXECUTE!**

*Build a strong circle of people around you, who are progressive, they think like you, challenge you to greatness and lift you up when you fall down!*

# TABLE OF CONTENTS

**INTRODUCTION** ................................................................ 5

**CHAPTER #1** ..................................................................... 1

**OVERVIEW: LEGISLATION & PROGRAMS** ......................... 1
- Legislation Supporting Women ........................................... 3
- Annual Spending Goals ...................................................... 4
- Women Owned Small Business (WOSB) Program ............... 5
- Why Legislation Is Important ............................................. 7
- Doing Business As .............................................................. 8
- The NAICS Codes .............................................................. 10
- FINDING YOUR CODES .................................................... 11
- WOSB and EDWOSB NAICS codes .................................... 14
- Case Example: ................................................................... 15
- Chapter #1: Summary ....................................................... 16
- Your Actions Steps: ........................................................... 17

**CHAPTER# 2: REGISTRATION** ........................................ 18
- Role of The Small Business Administration (SBA) ............. 18
- Registration Steps ............................................................. 19
- System For Award Management ....................................... 19
- Sam Checklist .................................................................... 20
- SBA's Office of Government Contracting (GC) .................. 22
- Certificate Of Competency (COC) ...................................... 23
- Your Business Size ............................................................ 24
- Small Business Size Standards ......................................... 24
- Chapter #2: Summary ....................................................... 25

**CHAPTER #3: CERTIFICATIONS** ...................................... 26
- Certification Overview ...................................................... 26
- Why Certify Your Business? .............................................. 27
- SBA Rules: Certification .................................................... 29
- SBA Certifications: US Small Business Administration ..... 32
- Case Example ................................................................... 33
- Chapter #3: Summary ....................................................... 34

**CHAPTER #4: CONTRACTING KNOWLEDGE** ................... 35
- Federal Acquisition Regulations (FAR) .............................. 35
- Forecasting Reports .......................................................... 37
- Laws and Small Business Concerns .................................. 38
- Prime Vs Subcontracting ................................................... 39
- Contracting Considerations .............................................. 39

Prime Contracting .................................................................. 40
Subcontracting As An Option .............................................. 41
Your Role As A Subcontractor ............................................. 42
Federal Compliance For Contractors .................................. 42
Compliance Requirements: E-Verify .................................. 44
Terminology And Acronyms ................................................ 44
Chapter #4: Summary ......................................................... 45

## CHAPTER #5 CONTRACTING VEHICLES AND TRENDS ........ 46
Contracting Vehicles ........................................................... 46
Leveraging Contracting Vehicles ........................................ 47
Sole Source Contracts ........................................................ 48
Contracting Trends: Best In Class ...................................... 49
Section #5: Chapter Summary ............................................ 51

## CHAPTER #6: ONLINE DATABASES ............................................. 52
Listing of Government Databases ...................................... 52
Summary: Databases .......................................................... 61
Chapter #6: Summary ......................................................... 64

## CHAPTER #7: FEDERAL GRANTS ............................................... 65
Federal Grants For Business Owners ................................. 65
Special Grant Programs ..................................................... 66
The America's Seed Fund ................................................... 66
The SBIR Program .............................................................. 67
The STTR Program ............................................................. 67
Grant for Business and Non-Profits ................................... 69
Chapter #7: SUMMARY ...................................................... 72

## CHAPTER #8: SUPPLIER DIVERSITY .......................................... 73
Overview of Supplier Diversity ........................................... 73
Why Supplier Diversity ....................................................... 73
Do You Qualify As A Diverse Supplier ............................... 74
Your Strategy ...................................................................... 75
Case Studies: Supplier Diversity ........................................ 76
Case Studies: Learning Tips .............................................. 82
Chapter #8: Summary ........................................................ 85

## CHAPTER # 9: CONTRACT READY ............................................. 86
Contract Ready Checklist ................................................... 86
Contracting Strategies ....................................................... 87
Contracting Options: Teaming And Joint Ventures ........... 87
Teaming And Federal Contracts ........................................ 88

Scope of Work Document ............................................................. 91
Scope of Work: Case Example .................................................... 91
RFP Steps For A Prime Contract ................................................ 94
Pricing And Contracts ................................................................ 96
Contract Considerations ............................................................ 96
Chapter #9: Summary ............................................................. 100

# CHAPTER #10: ACTION STEPS ............................................ 101
Contracting Plan of Action (CPA) ............................................ 101
Communication: Scripts .......................................................... 102
Prospecting .............................................................................. 102
Contract Diversification .......................................................... 104
Marketing Tool: Capability Statements .................................. 105
Chapter #10: Summary ........................................................... 108

# CHAPTER #11: HUMAN SIDE OF BUSINESS ...................... 109
Networking .............................................................................. 109
Networking Strategy ............................................................... 111
Building Trust ......................................................................... 112
Expand Your Reach With Social Media .................................. 113
Your Circle .............................................................................. 114
Your Value Proposition ........................................................... 115
Real Talk: Frequently Asked Questions ................................. 117

# APPENDICES .......................................................................... 121
Acronyms: Federal Contracting ............................................... 122
Glossary of Terms ................................................................... 125
Sections: Federal Bid Package ............................................... 132
Federal Unsolicited Proposal Format ..................................... 133
Form: Request for Quotation .................................................. 137
Form: Solicitation, Offer & Award .......................................... 138

# BUSINESS RESOURCE GUIDE .............................................. 139
Small Business Administration .............................................. 139
Small Business Development Centers (SBDC) ...................... 141
Office of Small and Disadvantaged Business Utilization (OSDBU) .... 142
Score-Core of Retired Executives ........................................... 146
Minority Business Development Agency (MBDA) ................. 147
Microloans Programs .............................................................. 148
Online Business Resources ..................................................... 150

# CHAPTER #1
# OVERVIEW: LEGISLATION & PROGRAMS

> This section provides you with some interesting statistics and information regarding legislation that specifically targets the growth and advancement of women in business. Educate yourself about programs that can be beneficial as a strategy to identify potential contract and business opportunities.

**Overview**

The workforce is changing and the number of women exploring the opportunity to start a business is increasing. Women are launching businesses to control their economic futures and have increased flexibility with their families. Economic factors including long term unemployment, downsizing and lack of career advancement also are a major factor. Women, especially women of color, are experiencing long-term unemployment and are pursuing business as a way out of poverty and the opportunity to increase their incomes.

Statistics confirm the rapid growth of women owned businesses and female entrepreneurs in the United States and abroad. There are numerous studies regarding women in business that reveal some interesting facts and figures. Let's examine a recent report commissioned by American Express titled "The 2018 State of Women Owned Business Report that studied business trends and compares the growth of women owned firms with that of men owned firms. The report confirms the following:

- As of 2018, women of color account for 47% of all women owned businesses. An estimated 5,824,300 women-of color-owned businesses employ 2,230,600 people and generate $386.6 billion in revenues.

- In 2018, women owned businesses that generated revenues less than 100,000 Were the vast majority — 10,775,600 or 88% — of all women-owned businesses.

- Over the past 20 years (1997–2017), the number of women-owned businesses has grown 114% compared to the overall national growth rate of 44% for all businesses.

- Women-owned businesses now account for 39% of all U.S. firms, employ 8% of the total private sector workforce and contribute 4.2% of total business revenues.

- The combination of women-owned businesses and firms equally-owned by men and women account for 47% of all businesses. These firms employ 14% of the workforce and generate 7% of revenues.

- The share of women-owned firms has grown much faster by number of firms than by employment and revenues.

- While the number of women-owned businesses grew 58% from 2007 to 2018, firms owned by women of color grew at nearly three times that rate (163%). Numbers for Latinas and African Americans grew even faster:

The report discusses the important economic impact and contributions that women business owners make to the overall economy. It also emphasizes the need for women in

business to have continued support, mentorship, access to capital and strong networks. Therefore, this book is designed educate women about programs and support networks that are designed to support business growth with contract opportunities.

As a women in business, you can benefit from designated programs with the Federal government and in the private sector. If you are seeking contracts in the private sector you should be aware of supplier diversity initiatives. If you are pursuing contracts with the federal government, you should understand federal legislation, including the business certifications provided by the Small Business Administration (SBA). The overall goal is for you to create multiple streams of income from a combination of contract opportunities with the federal government, counties, cities, municipalities, corporations and anchor institutions.

When you start a business, it is your intention for the business to be profitable and sustainable. Securing contract opportunities in the public and private sector is a way to earn revenue for your business enterprise. A necessary preparation for your success as a business owner and entrepreneur is to educate yourself. Therefore, this chapter includes an overview of legislation and the role of the Small Business Administration (SBA).

**Legislation Supporting Women**

The federal government fosters and supports women, minorities, and veterans with legislation and special programs. In the Small Business Act of July 30, 1953, Congress created the Small Business Administration (SBA),

whose function was to aid, counsel, assist and protect the interests of small business concerns. In 1969 President Nixon signed an executive order, which required government agencies and their contractors to provide opportunities for minority owned firms. This legislation required agencies to report results and establish goals. The SBA is also responsible for the oversight of federal contacts to ensure that small businesses are provided with a fair and equal opportunity to bid on, win and be awarded federal contracts. Executive orders and federal legislation were established to ensure that minority-owned firms were included in opportunities to bid on government projects as prime or subcontractors.

The Small Business Act authorizes contracting officers to specifically limit, or set aside, certain requirements for competition solely among women-owned small businesses (WOSBs) or economically disadvantaged women owned small businesses (EDWOSBs). The programs require a business to be at least 51% directly and unconditionally owned and controlled by one or more women who are citizens (born or naturalized) of the United States. The EDWOSB program requires that the business is owned and controlled by one or more women, each with a personal net worth less than $750,000. The eligibility requirements to qualify as a WOSB or an EDWOSB are fully defined in Title 13 Part 127 Subpart B of the Code of Federal Regulations (CFR). You can also get a preliminary assessment of whether you qualify at the SBA's Certify website: https://certify.sba.gov.

The Women's Business Ownership Act passed in 1988, provided recognition for women in business with additional resources and addressed discriminatory lending practices. The result of this legislation will insure that women have greater access to lending, business coaching and business training. Further supporting women in business was the creation of a national network of Women's Business Centers (WBC's) supported with funding from the Small Business Administration (SBA). The SBA Women's Business Centers provide technical assistance and resources to help women start, grow and expand their business enterprises. Women's Business Centers are located in various cities. For a comprehensive listing of Women Business Centers (WBC), you can visit the SBA website at **www.sba.gov** and search for Women's Business Centers.

## Annual Spending Goals

You should also know that the federal government sets annual spending goals for Women Owned Small Businesses. The following is a sample of the goals:

- 23% of prime contracts for small businesses
- 5% of prime and subcontracts for women-owned small businesses
- 5% of prime contracts and subcontracts for Small Disadvantaged Businesses
- 3% of prime contracts and subcontracts for HUBZone small businesses

- 3% of prime and subcontracts for service-disabled veteran-owned small businesses

The Small Business Administration (SBA) provides oversight to federal agencies to insure goals are met and reviews the performance of Federal agencies. The SBA only reviews performance of federal agencies and not private entities. However, if a private company is awarded a federal contract, the company is required to submit subcontracting plan to ensure that goals for minority and women owned businesses are accomplished. The SBA has a subcontracting website for entities receiving prime contracts. The following information is outlined on the SBA's site:

*"The mission of the program is to ensure that domestic small businesses receive a "maximum practical opportunity", which is a fair and equitable opportunity, to compete for and receive subcontracts resulting from Federal prime contracts. The purpose is also to ensure that other than small businesses (OTSB) understand and is in compliance with the subcontracting post-award legislations, regulations, processes, and procedures."*

Understanding the SBA's small business program creates opportunities to qualify for federal contracts. For example, if a major corporation receives a contract from the federal government, they are required to meet small business contracting goals for women and minority owned companies. You can leverage your certification as a Women Owned Small Business to help companies reach their goals.

*Source:* www.sba.gov

**Women Owned Small Business (WOSB) Program**

The WOSB Federal contracting program was implemented in February 2011 with the goal of expanding opportunities for WOSBs to win Federal contracts by providing a level playing field for WOSBs to compete. It is also intended to assist Federal agencies to meet the contracting goals for WOSBs. The Program allows WOSBs to compete for set-aside contracts or receive sole source awards in industries where women-owned small businesses are substantially underrepresented. It also enables economically disadvantaged WOSB's and EDWOSB's to compete for set-aside contracts or receive sole source awards in industries where women-owned small businesses are underrepresented. SBA is responsible for implementing and administering the Programs.

**What you need to know about the WOSB program:**

- The WOSB Program relies upon a self-certification process. Firms may self-certify as a WOSB or an EDWOSB by uploading all the required documentation to Certify.SBA.gov and updating your status as a WOSB or an EDWOSB on SAM.gov.
- New SBA rules will impact the self-certification process for WOSB and EDWOSB. Visit the Federal Register to stay updated on any changes.
- A company must be at least 51% directly and unconditionally owned and controlled by one or more women who are U.S. citizens.
- Set-asides and sole source awards are permitted under the WOSB Program.
- The set aside or sole source procurement must be in the industries designated by SBA as underrepresented.
- SBA has designated six-digit North American Industry Classification System (NAICS) codes to denote the industries where WOSBs are underrepresented.
- WOSB's and EDWOSB's can compete for contract awards under other socioeconomic programs if they meet the program requirements.
- There are no caps on the dollar amounts for set-aside contracts under the WOSB Program.

- Contracting officers, not SBA, are responsible for verifying that offerors have provided all the required documents to Certify.SBA.gov for WOSB or EDWOSB procurements.

For additional detailed information regarding the women owned small business programs, visit the small business administration website at (sba.gov). The SBA site contains detailed information regarding NAICS codes, certification requirements and other valuable information.

www.sba.gov

## Why Legislation Is Important

It is important to make yourself aware of the laws and legislation that can support you as a business owner. The federal government is one of the largest purchasers of goods and sets procurement goals for women owned small businesses every year. Take time to do your research and understand the processes, rules, laws and policies. The federal government has programs that support small business participation with the procurement process. This book will also include a discussion of the following important topics for women seeking contracts with the federal government:

- ➢ Set Asides and sole source acquisitions for Small Business
- ➢ Subcontracting plan requirements for prime contractors
- ➢ Socioeconomic programs

- Service disabled, and Veterans Owned Small Business procurement programs
- SBA and third-party certifications
- Contracting Vehicles
- Marketing strategies

**Doing Business As**

As you consider your options for contract and business opportunities, you don't have to have a brick and mortar business to pursue a contract opportunity. However, it would be advisable to set yourself up professionally to demonstrate that you are serious about doing business. For example, you can work with a prime contractor on a project as a Independent Contractor or a subcontractor. The following is a listing of entrepreneurial styles:

- Solopreneur
- Independent Contractor
- Consultant/Freelancer
- External Consultant

Which one of the definitions describes your business style?

**Solopreneur**
An entrepreneur that works alone in a business is a solopreneur. For example, a massage therapist is a great example of a solopreneur. Basically, a solopreneur can market their talents and skills and build a business that consist of one person.

**Independent Contractor**
The Internal Revenue Service Center describes an Independent Contractor as doctors, dentists, veterinarians, lawyers, accountants, contractors, subcontractors, public stenographers, or auctioneers who are in an independent trade, business, or profession in which they offer their services to the public.

The general rule is that an individual is an independent contractor if the payer has the right to control or direct only the result of the work and not what will be done and how it will be done. The earnings of a person who is working as an independent contractor are subject to Self-Employment Taxes.

If you are an independent contractor, you are self-employed and required to comply to tax obligations. To find out what your tax obligations are, visit the self-employed tax center on the Internal Revenue Service (IRS) website. You are not an independent contractor if you perform services that can be controlled by an employer (what will be done and how it will be done). This applies even if you are given freedom of action. What matters is that the employer has the legal right to control the details of how the services are performed.

If an employer-employee relationship exists (regardless of what the relationship is called), you are not an independent contractor and your earnings are generally not subject to Self-Employment Tax.

**Consultant/Freelancer**

According to the Bureau of Labor Statistics, in 2015, 15.5 million people in the United States were self-employed and the number continues to grow rapidly. A consultant provides expert advice in a specialized field. There is a new economy emerging and work patterns are changing. Mobile devices and smartphones has also created opportunities to work from home and connect globally. In the business circle, working as a "Consultant" is a unique opportunity to share your professional expertise in a specific field.

**External consultant** - someone who is employed externally to the client usually by a firm or agency on a temporary basis for a fee. Entrepreneurs can work from a home-based business and can provide services to business as a

consultant. The following is an example of areas that consultants provide advice:
- Management

- Accounting and Bookkeeping
- Computer
- Information Technology
- Technical Writing
- Human Resources
- Marketing
- Public Relations
- Engineering
- Finances
- Science
- Health

Marketing your skills as a Consultant is a great opportunity for you to build a profitable business enterprise. As a Consultant, you can offer your skills in a specific area of your expertise. Carefully assess your skills and the professional areas that you can provide expertise. For example, if you have ten years of experience working as a Fundraiser for a large nonprofit, then you can lend your skills as a Fundraiser to other organizations. Perhaps you have years of experience working on marketing campaigns, you can serve as a consultant on marketing projects. Basically, take an assessment of your skills, background and experience that would make you a valuable Consultant in the private or public sector. You can still work with prime contractors seeking to identify Independent Contractors, Freelancers and Consultants to complete a scope of the work as part of the contract.

**The NAICS Codes**

As an entrepreneur, you need to know your NAICS Codes! It is important that you know and understand these numbers because they are the codes that describe your business industry. Remember, the federal government is not the only entity that utilizes NAICS codes. You will be asked for your codes on various business applications and credit forms. You will discover that states, cities, and other political entities utilize SBA's size standards based on NAICS for their procurement programs.

I get asked this question all of the time – what is a NAICS CODE? Ironically, some of the entrepreneurs that are beginning to pursue government contracts have no idea about the codes. The North American Industry Classification System (NAICS) codes were developed by the Office of Management and Budget (OMB) --in 1997 to replace SIC or the Standard Industrial Classification system. The United States Census Bureau and other federal statistical agencies use NAICS codes for collecting and reporting economic data. Entities utilizing NAICS codes includes states, cities, and political subdivisions (*e.g.*, airport and bridge authorities) use or adapt SBA's size standards based on NAICS for their procurement programs. Federal and non-federal entities use NAICS codes for administrative and tax purposes. For example, the U.S. Department of Transportation provides reduced registration fees for a small business; but those businesses must identify their NAICS code when they apply for the reduced fee.

**FINDING YOUR CODES**

**You can go directly to the site** www.census.com and put in keywords that describe your business. You can also visit the United States Census Bureau NAICS website to identify your NAICS code(s). You can search this site by a keyword that describes your industry. We recommend using a single word in the search box that is suitable for your business. To find the code for your business industry you can visit the following website: www.census.gov/naics.

The screenshot above is a sample of the United States Census Bureau website. This is a great site for you to research possible NAICS codes for your business. You can search for your code with a keyword that identifies your business industry. For example, if you input the term Marketing, the page will populate with NAICS codes for marketing areas. You should spend time selecting all the applicable NAICS codes that reflect your business activities.

This is a great resource site to research your NAICS codes. There is a great help section that will answer any questions related to the codes. On the site, you can find answers to all of the following questions:

1. **What is NAICS and how is it used?**
2. **What is an establishment?**
3. **What are "statistical purposes?"**
4. **What is a "primary business activity?"**
5. **What is the NAICS structure and how many digits are in a NAICS code?**
6. **I have seen NAICS codes with more than six digits. What are these, and how can I get a list of them?**
7. **Where can I get a complete list of 2017 NAICS codes?**

8. What is the Standard Industrial Classification (SIC) system? Is it still being used?
9. How can I determine the correct NAICS code for my business?
10. Who assigns NAICS codes to businesses and how?
11. How can I have my company's NAICS code changed?
12. How can I get a new NAICS code created for my type of business?
13. How does NAICS 2017 differ from NAICS 2012?
14. Do NAICS codes change over time?
15. Can a business have more than one NAICS code?
16. How do the NAICS codes affect federal procurement and regulatory activities, such as those carried out by the Environmental Protection Agency, the Occupational Safety and Health Administration (OSHA), the Department of Defense, and the General Services Administration?
17. What is the relationship between NAICS and the Small Business Administration's (SBA) size standards?
18. How can I find an occupational NAICS code?
19. How can I find data (payroll, number of establishments, sales, receipts, etc.) for a specific NAICS industry?
20. Are U.S. international trade data available on a NAICS basis?
21. How does NAICS handle market-based rather than production-based statistical classifications?
22. What is Title 13?
23. How can I download the NAICS manual?
24. How do NAICS codes relate to other classification systems?
25. My company is overseas. What is my NAICS code?
26. If my question isn't here or I still need more information, what should I do?

## WOSB and EDWOSB NAICS codes

As a strategy for increasing the number of opportunities for Women Owned Small business, The WOSB program has identified specific NAICS codes where women owned small businesses are underrepresented as recipients of government contract awards. The codes cover a range of industries. A full listing of the applicable NAICS codes can be reviewed at: www.sba.gov/wosb.

SUPPORT

## Qualifying NAICS for the Women-Owned Small Business Federal Contracting program

*Effective Oct 1, 2017*

*The SBA regularly maintains the list of NAICS that can qualify for the women's contracting program.*

The arrow on the screen shot demonstrates where you can click to download the report. You can visit the SBA site to get an updated list of the NAICS codes for Women Owned Small Businesses (WOSB's) and Economically Disadvantaged Women Owned Small Business (EDWOSB's). The NAICS codes for the WOSB program were identified through a study, which examined the "disparity ratio" between WOSBs utilized in Federal contracting for a particular NAICS code. If the ratio was 0.8 or less, WOSBs are considered underrepresented. Since the law requires that a study be conducted to identify the codes, there is no appeal process to designate additional NAICS codes as underrepresented.

There are specific codes for Women Owned Small Businesses (WOSB's) and Economically Disadvantaged Women Owned Small Businesses (EDWOSB's). You can visit the Small Business Administration (SBA) website to get a complete listing of the NAICS codes. You can google "WOSB NAICS Codes" or "EDWOSB NAICS codes". A pdf file from the SBA will populate that will list the six digit number and description for the NAICS codes.

Congratulations, you have taken the first step to prepare for contracting. Remember, NAICS codes are utilized by other industries on vendor applications. Do your research and make sure you select all the NAICS codes that are applicable for your business. Also, you should keep your SAM profile updated with all of your selected codes. Remember, the primary NAICS code selected for your business should represent the largest segment of your business income. You can select additional codes for other products or services that you will offer.

**Case Example:**

Lisa just started a graphic design business and wants to pursue federal contracts. She visited the census.gov site and entered the keyword (graphic Design). the code for graphic design "541613" immediately popped up in the right column. Lisa is also interested in integrating marketing management as a part of her business. She identified another code "541613" for Marketing Management Consulting Services as another code for the work provided from her company. As Lisa grows her business, she will keep her SAM profile updated with additional services or products that she will provide as part of her business. You can select multiple NAICS Codes to identify the services you offer as part of your business.

# Chapter #1: Summary

- Executive orders and federal legislation is designed to ensure minorities and women owned businesses have equal opportunities for contract opportunities.

- Federal agencies establish annual spending and contracting goals in consultation with the Small Business Administration (SBA).

- Businesses are required to meet specific criteria to qualify for certification as a WOSB or EDWOSB.

- The WOSB and EDWOSB are certification programs administered by the Small Business Administration (SBA).

- The North American Industry Classification Code System (NAICS) is a numbering system that identifies your business industry. You can select more than one NAICS Codes for your business.

- Visit the census bureau site to search and identify your NAICS codes and get additional information.

- NAICS codes are also utilized by other entities including state, local governments and organizations for procurement programs.

- There are specific NAICS codes for the WOSB and EDWOSB programs. Visit sba.gov to get a completing listing of the applicable codes for the WOSB and EDWOSB programs.

**Your Actions Steps:**

Go to www.census.gov/NAICS, put in your keywords, review the descriptions and carefully identify NAICS codes for your business.

What is your primary NAICS Codes?

1) _____

List three other NAICS codes that could be applicable to your business industry

    1) _____
    2) _____
    3) _____
    4) _____
    5) _____

- Do you have a Dun & Bradstreet number? If not, go to Dun & Bradstreet to apply for a number
- Research SBA certifications and select the ones applicable to your business
- Begin writing your capability statement
- Review the listing of SBA certifications and make start the process to obtain the ones that are applicable to your business. You should begin with the WOSB and the EDWOSB.

# CHAPTER# 2: REGISTRATION

> Before you pursue contracts with the federal government, take time to plan and prepare. The first step is registering your business in the System for Award Management (SAM) online portal. You should also familiarize yourself with important terminology related specifically to Federal contracting.

**Role of The Small Business Administration (SBA)**

When you think about doing business, The U.S. Small Business Administration (SBA) has always been one of the agencies that has served as a great resource for entrepreneurs. Created in 1953, The SBA has delivered millions of loans, loan guarantees, contracts, counseling sessions and other forms of assistance to businesses. As outlined on SBA's website, the agency provides assistance through the following four core program areas:

- **Access to Capital**
  The SBA does not provide loans directly to businesses, however, they work with lenders to help small business owners secure loans. The agency sets guidelines for loans made by community development organizations, partnering lenders and micro lending institutions.

- **Technical Assistance & Training**
  Entrepreneurs and business owners can visit one of the SBA's 1800 locations for training, coaching and specialized workshops on a range of business topics. Further assistance is available through the SBA SCORE chapters, Women's Business Centers and Small Business Development Center's (SBDC's).

- **Resources for Prime and Subcontracting Opportunities**
  The Federal government has set contracting goals that are mandated by

law in Section 15(g) of the Small Business Act. Federal departments and agencies work annually to reach the statutory goal of 23 percent in prime contract dollars to small businesses.

- **Advocacy**

    Working on your behalf is the SBA's "Office of Advocacy", which serves as an independent voice for small business within the federal government and the watchdog for the Regulatory Flexibility Act (RFA). Advocacy efforts advance the views and concerns of small business before Congress, the White House, the federal agencies, the federal courts and state policy makers. For additional information visit: www.sba.gov/advocacy.

## Registration Steps

As you pursue potential contract opportunities, you need to complete the necessary registration steps required by each entity. Most companies will have online portals and they will require you to register your business in their online portal as a vendor/supplier. The registration process for doing business with the federal government is different from the private sector. If you want to do business with the federal government, registering your business in the System for Award Management (SAM) is the first step. If you do not register your business in SAM, you are not eligible to do business with the federal government.

## System For Award Management

The System for Award Management (SAM) is the official U.S. government online database that contains data for potential contractors and suppliers. When you register your business in SAM, you are automatically included in a database and this information is available to various government agencies. There is no fee to register for this site and you can register at no cost directly at **www.sam.gov**. Before your register, check the URL to make sure that you are at the official secured SAM site with .gov at the end. The following is a screen shot of the SAM website:

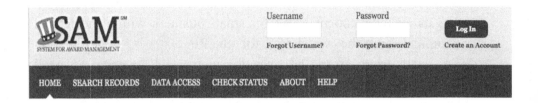

The SAM Registration can be a complex process if you have no prior contracting knowledge. Go to the help section and click on the User Guides and read the helpful hints. The *help section* provides a Non-Federal User Guide that you can download in a pdf format, or you can also access the guide online. Before you start the registration process, it is important that you utilize these guides to acquire an understanding of the basic terminology and how to answer the questions. The site also includes a SAM Overview Video.

**Sam Checklist**

### SYSTEM FOR AWARD MANAGEMENT CHECKLIST

How to register in SAM
1. Go to SAM website: www.sam.gov
2. Create a SAM user account and verify your email
3. Register New Entity under "Register/Update Entity on our "My SAM" page
4. Choose the purpose of your registration

Document Checklist
1. DUNS Number
2. NAICS CODES
3. FSC (Federal Supply Class) & PSC (Product Service Code) optional
4. Date & location of incorporation
5. 5) EIN (Federal Employer Identification Number)

5. Enter your information Core Data
6. Fill out the option for SBA profile
7. Review your information and click on submit your registration

6. Bank account routing number, credit card information and contact information
7. Business fiscal year, business start date, fiscal year end date
8. Point of contact information

SAM now requires a *notarized letter* stating that you are the authorized Entity Administrator. The website provides an example of the letter to be included during the registration process. The following pages outline the SAM database, documentation required and the process.

Here are a few things that you should know about SAM:

Currently, the Duns Number is required to register in SAM, however, A notice was published in the Federal Register regarding the DUNS Number. Beginning in December 2020, the D-U-N-S® number will no longer be the official identifier for conducting business with the U.S. Government.

The System for Award Management (SAM) is an official website of the U.S. government. You can register for free and there is no cost to use the SAM –here is what you can do at the site:

- Register to do business with the US government
- Update or renew your entity registration
- Check the status of an entity registration
- Search for entity registration and records

The following is a screenshot of what you will see when you visit the site.

If you have any problems, you can to to the help section and review a user guide – see below:

| Help | User Guides |
|---|---|
| | Quick User Guides |
| User Guides | **Helpful Hints for Entity Registrations** |
| Quick User Guides | **Description:** Guidance for registrants on understanding your entity's registration status. |
| Full User Guides | VIEW Understanding Your Entity's Registration Status |
| Helpful Hints | |
| | **Description:** Using SAM with the help of a Screen Reader. |
| International Registrants | DOWNLOAD PDF Best practice tips for using Screen Readers to navigate the SAM website |
| Demonstration Videos | |
| Exclusions Information | **Quick Start Guide for Service Contract Reporting (SCR)** |
| External Resources | |
| | **Description:** A short reference guide to help you report on your Service Contracts for the previous Government fiscal year |

## SBA's Office of Government Contracting (GC)

There are other divisions of the SBA that provides special programs to assist small businesses. The SBA's office of Government Contracting is dedicated to the mission of assisting small businesses with obtaining a fair share of Federal Government contracts, subcontracts and property sales. The GC Office works closely with contracting staff and federal buying offices to set aside contract opportunities for all categories. Other activities include providing training to federal agencies, resource partners and small businesses. Overall, The GC Offices engage in a range of activities which includes monitoring, training and counseling to insure small businesses get their share of contracts. One of the programs conducted by the GC office is the certificate of competency program (COC).

**Certificate Of Competency (COC)**

The Certificate of Competency Program (COC) is designed

to determine if a small business meets the qualifications for a contract. The program allows for a small business to appeal a contracting officer's determination that it is unable to fulfill the requirements of a government contract. The program provides the opportunity for a small business to acquire a thorough review of the circumstances and, if applicable, issue a certificate of competency on behalf of the contractor to the contracting officer. Basically, if a Small Business is determined "non-responsible" for a specific contract, the business can appeal the findings and request a "Certificate Of Competency" review. If this occurs a contract is withheld for 15 business days to provide time for the SBA to investigate. The applicant must be able to demonstrate that it is sufficiently responsible to perform on the contract.

*Visit the sba.gov for additional information regarding the COC process*

The Government Contracting (GC) Office is organized in six (6) area offices in the following states: Boston, Washington DC, Atlanta, Chicago, Dallas/Fort Worth and San Francisco. The following is a list of the overall programs conducted under the GC Offices:

- Prime Contracts and Procurement Center Representative (PCR) Program
- Commercial Market Representative (CMR) program
- Certification of Competency Program (COC) program
- Size Program
- Natural Resource & Sales Assistance Program (Timber)

The (SBA) in continually working on the behalf of small businesses to insure equal access to prime and subcontracting opportunities. The range of programs are designed to assist and help businesses grow and develop.

**Your Business Size**

In preparation for federal contracting, it is important for you to understand some basic information as it relates to your business. If you meet small business standards you can qualify for set asides, small business contracts, SBA loans programs that are specifically targeted for women and minority owned small businesses. Government agencies set specific goals to do business with entities classified as "small business". The prime and subcontracting goals are established for small businesses, small businesses owned by women, small disadvantaged businesses, service-disabled veteran-owned small businesses, and small businesses located in Historically Underutilized Business Zones (HUBZone's*).*

**Small Business Size Standards**

A size standard, which is usually classified based on the number of employees or average annual receipts, represents the largest size that a business (including its subsidiaries and affiliates) may be to remain classified as a small business for SBA and federal contracting programs. The definition of "small" varies by industry. To help small business owners assess their small business status, SBA has established a Table of Small Business Size Standards which is matched to the North American Industry Classification System (NAICS) for industries. Certain government programs, such as SBA loan programs and contracting opportunities, are reserved for small business concerns. In order to qualify, businesses must satisfy SBA's definition of a small business concern, along with the size standards for small businesses

# Chapter #2: Summary

- The SBA provides entrepreneurs with assistance in the following core areas: access to capital, technical assistance, resources for prime/subcontracting opportunities and advocacy.

- The System for Award Management (SAM) is the official U.S. government online database that contains data for potential contractors and suppliers.

- If you are not registered in SAM, you cannot do business with the federal government.

- Small Businesses can get additional assistance from The Government Contracting (GC) Office. There is a GC office located in six (6) area offices in the following states: Boston, Washington DC, Atlanta, Chicago, Dallas/Fort Worth and San Francisco.

- The Commercial Market Representative (CMR) works in the SBA's Office of Government Contracting as a resource for entrepreneurs.

- Government agencies set specific goals to do business with entities classified as "small business".

- The Certification of Competency (COC) allows small businesses to request a review to determine the ability of their business to perform on a contract.

# CHAPTER #3: CERTIFICATIONS

> Certifications play an important role for women owned businesses. Obtaining a certification is a strategy that can be utilized as an advantage for women and economically disadvantaged groups. However, there is a lot of confusion around the certification process. It is a good idea research your options and develop a certification strategy.

**Certification Overview**

The question that you should ask yourself is "what companies/entities would I like to pursue for contract opportunities?" If you are seeking to do business with a local city government, it would be wise to research what registration and certifications are required. If you would like to pursue contracts from federal agencies, you should certify with the Small Business Administration (SBA). Remember, you are first required to register your business in SAM before you can obtain a certification from the SBA. The certifications you acquire should carefully align with your business strategy.

A certified supplier is one that has gone through a certification process offered through the U.S. Small Business or an agency referred to as a third party. The process requires you to submit specific documentation to confirm that your business is a minority businesses enterprise (MBE), Lesbian, Gay, Bisexual or (LGBT) women-owned small business (WOSB), women business enterprise (WBE), small disadvantaged businesses (SDB), or a veteran-owned businesses (VOSB).

There are several ways that you can certify your business:

1) Do it yourself with the Small Business Administration (SBA) website: certify.sba.gov

2) Approved SBA third party certification agencies

3) Certify as a Minority Business Enterprise (MBE) from your local state or city

4) Disadvantaged Business Enterprise (DBE) from Department of Transportation (DOT)

5) Certify with the National Minority Supplier Development Council (NMSDC) as a Minority Owned Business

The Following is a list of organizations approved to serve as Third Party Certifiers under the WOSB Program:

- El Paso Hispanic Chamber of Commerce
- National Women Business Owners Corporation
- US Women's Chamber of Commerce
- Women's Business Enterprise National Council (WBENC)

Third Party certifiers will charge a fee for services and you are required to renew every year. The certification process for third party certifiers includes a series of screenings, interviews, and site visits to ensure that you are a minority and/or women-owned business. You will pay a standard fee for this certification service. However, you can opt to complete a do it yourself certification process with the U.S. Small Business Administration (SBA). The Small Business Administration has a site that will walk you through the certification process.

**Why Certify Your Business?**

Certification is a process that confirms that your business is owned, managed, and controlled by a qualifying diverse group. Special certifications will provide your company with an opportunity to be considered for contracts based upon your status as a woman, minority, or disadvantaged business owner. Corporations and agencies have programs that are specifically targeted for companies that are certified. It also helps companies monitor and track their progress with the number of certified companies that secure contract and business opportunities. Overall, certifying your business will help you qualify for additional opportunities that are designed to support women and minority owned concerns. As you think about doing business, utilize the certification process as an advantage to leverage your business for wider and broader opportunities.

Here is a question that you need to consider: do I need to get certified when I start a business? You need to analyze where you are in business and where you want to go. Doing research can help you build a case for what types of certifications would be advantageous to you as a business. You can start with the Do It Yourself certifications with the Small Business Administration (SBA). Visit certify.sba.gov to review the application process.

Here is your checklist of considerations:

- What certification are valued by a prospective buyer?
- Will the certification help me leverage my business for a contract opportunity?
- Is my business ready for the certification process?

You should do your research and choose the best certification process that will aligns with your business goals. You may want to start slow and master the FREE certification process with the U.S. Small Business Administration.

You can leverage your SBA certifications and status as a woman owned business when you are pursuing contracts with corporations and other industries. For example, Walmart's supplier diversity page outlines a list of the certifications that are recognized by Walmart. The list clearly states that certifications from federal and local governments will be recognized. Therefore, the SBA Women Owned Small Business (WOSB) and the Economically Disadvantaged Women Owned Small Business (EDWOSB) certifications are acknowledged by Walmart.

Certifications are an important strategy for your business. SBA certifications are important for pursuing contracts with the federal government. If you are pursuing contracts with corporations, counties, cities, states and other entities, do you research.

**SBA Rules: Certification**

It is extremely important to stay informed of policies that can have a direct impact on how you do business and understand what drives policy decisions. For example, the Small Business Administration is proposing to amend its regulations regarding the requirements to certify Women-Owned Small Business Concerns (WOSBs) and Economically Disadvantaged Women-Owned Small Business Concerns (EDWOSBs) participating in the Women-

Owned Small Business Contract Program. Currently there are numerous problems and compliance issues associated with the self-certification process in awarding contracts to WOSBs and EDWOSBs. In order to address these problems, the SBA is proposing new regulations. Under the new proposed regulations, the burden of eligibility and compliance will be with the SBA, a federal agency or an SBA approved third party national certifying entity.

As a Women Owned Small Business once you complete the System for Award (SAM) registration process on sam.gov, you have the option to self-certify your business. The self-certification process requires you to set up an online account at certify.sba.gov, upload the required documentation and complete the online questions. The portal allows you to certify as a Women Owned Small Business (WOSB) and as an Economically Disadvantaged Business (ED WOSB). Upon completion of the online registration process the system automatically generates a confirmation letter verifying your certification. The second option is to pay a fee to an SBA approved third party certifying agency.

**Below is a quick summary of some of the proposed changes as of (July, 2019):**

- After these rules are finalized, WOSBs that are not certified will not be eligible to compete on set asides.
- SBA will accept certifications that have been issued by SBA, a federal agency or State authority under the DOT/DBE program.
- The SBA proposes that the EDWOSB and 8(a) income eligibility guidelines match.
- All applications will be required to be registered in the System for Award Management (SAM) at sam.gov/SAM/ to qualify for WOSB, EDWOSB certifications.
- Small businesses will be certified by a Federal Agency, a State government or a national certifying agency in order to be awarded a set aside or sole source contract under the WOSB program.
- The SBA will continue to provide an online electronic application process

- Once you complete the application process you can no longer receive automatic approval, you must wait for your application to be approved and verified.
- After submitting your online application, there will be a waiting period for approval. If you submit an incomplete application the waiting period could take up to 90 days.

It is good to know that the SBA will also utilize existing government certification from the Federal and State levels that have valid certification programs in which the SBA could accept in lieu of an SBA only process. Examples of these certification programs from a federal agency include the Department of Transportation/Disadvantaged Business Enterprise (DOT/DBE) program.

SBA has will minimize the impact of new legislation by also accepting certifications already received from SBA, through Department of Transportation (DOT)'s Disadvantaged Business Enterprise (DBE) program or the Veterans Affairs (VA) Center for Veterans Enterprise (CVE) program. Businesses that are already certified by a third party will be allowed a one-year grace period for certification. Stay tuned for the dates the regulations will be implemented.

For a more detailed description of the proposed changes and regulations visit the federal register to stay informed of the changes and updates. As you proceed with deciding on what certifications to obtain, visit the websites of your prospective clients and review their policies, supplier diversity programs, registration processes and other information.

For example, if you want to do business with Walmart, visit Walmart's website and review information that outlines how they do business with vendors/suppliers. The information obtained from Walmart states that certifications from the following entities are also accepted:

- U.S. Small Business Administration (SBA)

- Veteran/Disabled Veterans (VOB)
- LGBT
- Accept self-certification form as part of the registration process
- Programs and certifications that can be beneficial for your business

## SBA Certifications: US Small Business Administration

**SBA certifications that can be beneficial for your business**

| TYPE | DESCRIPTION |
|---|---|
| WOSB Women Owned Small Business Program | The WOSB program authorizes contracting officers to set aside certain federal contracts for eligible women-owned small businesses. |
| Small Disadvantaged Businesses | Firms that are considered to be small disadvantaged businesses can compete for certain federal contracting opportunities. |
| 8(a) Business Development Program | The 8(a) Business Development Program was created to help small, disadvantaged businesses compete in the marketplace. The program offers a broad scope of assistance to companies owned and controlled at least 51% by socially and economically disadvantaged individuals. |
| Hub Zone | A program providing preferential access to federal procurement opportunities for businesses in urban and rural communities. |
| VOSB Veteran Owned Small Business | Veteran-Owned Small Businesses (VOSBs) are eligible to receive no less than 3% of the total annual value of all government prime and subcontract awards. |
| SDVOSB: Service-Disabled Veteran Owned Small Business | This procurement program allows federal contracting officers to set acquisitions aside, if certain conditions are met, SDVOSBs are also eligible for sole source awards. |

For additional information, visit **www.sba.gov** to obtain detailed information about each certification.

## Case Example

Paris started a Control design manufacturing company and operate with several NAICS CODES her business. We advised her to complete her research and make a list of the federal agencies and companies that she wanted to do business with. When she made her list, we further advised her to do her research, go to each of the websites. She know that she could utilize the federal agencies her WOSB certifications. Surprisingly, one of the companies that she targeted was Accenture. She went to the Supplier Diversity portal at Accenture and registered as a vendor supplier. She also thoroughly reviewed the entities that they accepted certifications from.

As a result of her research, discovered that the SBA certifications were acknowledged at Accenture. She also discovered that they had a division for doing business with the government. This also worked to her advantaged with her approach to the contracting officer at the company.

If you want to take advantage of federal certifications, you must complete the process required for the federal government. However, as stated in previous chapters, you have to register your business in the System for Award Management (SAM) before you can obtain a SBA certification.

## Chapter #3: Summary

- A certified supplier is one that has gone through a certification process offered through the U.S. Small Business or an agency referred to as a third party. The process requires the submission of specific documentation to confirm that the business is a minority businesses enterprise (MBE), Lesbian, Gay, Bisexual or (LGBT) women-owned small business (WOSB), women business enterprise (WBE), small disadvantaged businesses (SDB), or a veteran-owned businesses (VOSB).

- Certifications provide businesses with an opportunity to be considered for contracts based upon status as a woman, minority, or disadvantaged business owner.

- You can leverage SBA certifications and status as a woman owned business when pursuing contracts with corporations and other industries.

- New rules for the SBA will change the self certification process, you can still certify, however, there will be a waiting period for a decision.

- Conduct research and choose the best certification process that will aligns with your business goals. Visit the websites of prospects and review the list of certifications that are acknowledged by the company.

- You can leverage your SBA certifications as a woman owned business when you are pursuing contracts with corporations and other industries.

# CHAPTER #4: CONTRACTING KNOWLEDGE

> This section focuses on equipping you with knowledge to pursue contracts in the federal marketplace. When you acquire an understanding of the federal contracting process, you can easily master the process required for states, counties, schools and other entities. You should familiarize yourself with portions of the Federal Acquisition Regulation (FAR), a document that outlines policies and procedures for federal contracting.

**Federal Acquisition Regulations (FAR)**

The FAR is a standardized set of regulations used by all federal agencies when they are making purchases. It provides procedures for every step of the procurement process, from the time that the government discovers a need for a product or service to the time the purchase is complete.

When the government purchases products and services it requires suppliers to meet certain qualifications such as registration, Dun Bradstreet number, etc. There are also standardized procedures as outlined in the FAR, that govern the purchase of goods and services.

As a business owner or entrepreneur seeking to conduct business with the federal government, you should review and become familiar with the FAR. **www.acquisition.gov**.

The following is an example of topics are covered in FAR:

- ✓ Small Business participation in acquisitions
- ✓ Determination of Small Business Status for Small Business Programs
- ✓ Set Asides for Small Business concerns
- ✓ The Small Business Contracting Programs – Definitions
- ✓ Subcontracting Plan Requirements
- ✓ Determining the need for a subcontracting plan
- ✓ Preparing for a solicitation

- ✓ A thorough description of Small Business programs
- ✓ Partnership agreements

Here is a screen caption of Acquisition.gov

Federal Acquisition Regulation (FAR)

| FAR PARTS | Full FAR Download in Various Formats | | | | | | |
|---|---|---|---|---|---|---|---|
| Index | FAC Number | Effective Date | HTML | XML | PDF | Word | EPub |
| List of Sections Affected | FAC 2019-03 | 07-12-2019 | | | | | |

| | Browse FAR Part/Subpart and Download in Various Formats | | | |
|---|---|---|---|---|
| 1 2 3 4 5 6 | Parts/Subparts | HTML | XML | Print |
| 7 8 9 10 11 12 | | | | |
| 13 14 15 16 17 18 | | | | |
| 19 20 21 22 23 24 | | | | |
| 25 26 27 28 29 30 | Part 1 - Federal Acquisition Regulations System | | | |
| 31 32 33 34 35 36 | | | | |
| 37 38 39 40 41 42 | Subpart 1.1 - Purpose, Authority, Issuance | | | |
| 43 44 45 46 47 48 | | | | |
| 49 50 51 52 53 | Subpart 1.2 - Administration | | | |

*Please note the column to the left, the 53 FAR chapters

You don't have to be an expert or spend time reaching each of the chapters outlined in the FAR. However, the FAR is an invaluable resource for you to stay informed and understand the policies that guide federal contracting. Take your time, and first study the chapters outlined below:

Here is a listing of recommended chapters that you should review:

- ➤ Part #4: Administrative Matters
- ➤ Part #6: Competition Requirements
- ➤ Part #13: Simplified Acquisitions
- ➤ Part #16: Types of Contracts
- ➤ Part #19: Small Business Programs

## Forecasting Reports

The question explored by entrepreneurs and small business owners is *"where can I find contract opportunities"*? We will discuss research strategies that will be useful for tracking prime and sub-contracting opportunities. In chapter #1, there is a discussion of the laws, regulations and federal goals for contracting with women and minority owned companies. There are also laws that require federal agencies to list projected procurement opportunities. Below is a summary of the Business Opportunity Development Reform Act of 1988:

*Public Law 100-656, the Business Opportunity Development Reform Act of 1988, amended the Small Business Act to emphasize acquisition planning. The law requires agencies to compile and make available projections of contracting opportunities that small, minority and women-owned businesses may be able to perform. We also extend our efforts to provide opportunities for Historically Underutilized Business Zone (HUBZone) small businesses and Service-Disabled Veteran-Owned (SDVO) small businesses. HUBZone and SDVO small businesses are encouraged to market their capabilities to Treasury to assist us with our various small business acquisition strategies.*

An invaluable website are reports posted on the acquisition.gov website. This is the online site to review "Agency Recurring Procurement Forecast" reports. From the home page, navigate down to the Business Zone Area. When you click on the Business Zone, you will be directed to the following four categories:

- Help Build the Acquisition Gateway!
- Category Management
- Product and Service Codes Manual
- Agency Recurring Procurement Forecasts
- The Procurement Technical Assistance Program (PTAP)

Click on "Agency Recurring Procurement Forecasts" and the page will populate with a listing of federal agencies. Click on the agencies to view information related to projected contract opportunities. Each of the agencies will have a report and each agency will have different formats.

**Laws and Small Business Concerns**

As discussed in chapter #1, there are laws that require prime contractors receiving federal contracts to provide subcontracting opportunities for small businesses. As you pursue contracting opportunities, you may consider reaching out to prime contractors to explore subcontracting opportunities. For example, the passage of the National Defense Authorization Act (NDAA) authorized prime contractors to count the awarding of contracts to lower tier small business concerns (SBCS) to meet federal contracting goals. As stated in NDAA:

**NDAA Sec. 1614: Credit for Small Business Subcontractors:** This provision requires prime contractors to review and monitor their subcontractors' subcontracting plans to ensure compliance with stated goals. It also allows for the inclusion of lower-tier subcontractors for purposes of satisfying a prime contractor's small business goals. You can leverage your status as a Women Owned Small Business (WOSB) and prime contractors can count your participation to meet federal contracting goals.

The federal government operates in complete transparency when doing business. There are several valuable databases that can help you locate information related to upcoming, current and past contract opportunities. You can utilize this information to create a contracting plan of action (CPA). Your contracting plan of action should include a list of targeted companies, agencies, businesses, institutions or any company that will purchase your product or service.

Remember, you can become overwhelmed very quickly with loads of information, therefore, it may be advisable for you to narrow down your list of prospects and focus your attention to a limited number of prospects at a time.

**Prime Vs Subcontracting**

First, let's begin with federal contracting and assume that you are just getting started. I discuss in class how you can enter the federal contracting arena through the front door, side door or back door.

If you are ready to assume the full responsibility for a contract, you can enter through the front door and start

bidding on contracts as a Prime Contractor. You can come in the side door, as a subcontractor or Independent contractor and work on acquiring experience and building up your business capability. You can also enter through the back door as a sub to a sub-contractor, Freelancer, Consultant or Independent Contractor. Your contracting strategy should depend on where you are with your business. If you are new to the contracting arena, it may be a good idea to build your performance as a sub-contractor before you assume the entire responsibility for a contract.

**Contracting Considerations**

You can pursue a federal contract as a prime or subcontractor. A contracting strategy that you may want to consider is subcontracting. Perhaps you are not ready to assume the full financial or administrative responsibilities for a contract, subcontracting could be the answer. Here is a set of questions that we will refer to as your Strengths, Weaknesses, Opportunities and Threats (SWOT) analysis for contracting.

1. What are your business strengths?
2. Do you have past performance within your industry?
3. Can you provide a quality product/service to the prime contractor?
4. Can you meet all the deadlines outlined in the contract?

5. Do you have the staff resources and support to successfully complete the contract requirements?
6. Do you have the financial resources to support staff and contractors required for the contract?
7. Do you have adequate staffing to make someone from your company the lead on the contract?

**Prime Contracting**

It is important to understand the language of contracting and the differences with federal contracting vs. private contracting. In federal contracting, a Prime Contractor is a business entity that has been awarded a contract with the federal government as a result of completing a bid or responding to an RFP. Prime contractors assume the entire legal and financial responsibility for performing and completing the agreed scope of work that is outlined in the proposal.

As a prime contractor, you own the project and assume the full responsibility for the successful completion of the contract. When you assume a prime contract, you should have the processes in place to manage the entire project and assume the entire financial responsibility. Additionally, when you assume a federal contract, the government requires you to comply with specific laws and regulations. Here is a list of compliance standards for prime contractors awarded from the federal government:

- ✓ Implement internal procedures that comply with reaching affirmative action goals
- ✓ Integrate a tracing system for applicants
- ✓ Implement timekeeping and labor management processes
- ✓ Conduct E-verify confirmations
- ✓ If you are in construction, review requirements under Davis-Bacon Related Acts (DBRA)

- ✓ Maintain accurate employment payment records for three years
- ✓ Engage in outreach efforts that identify females, minorities and veterans

## Subcontracting As An Option

A "Subcontractor" is a company that enters into an agreement with a "Prime Contractor" to complete a portion of the scope of work outlined in the contract. The sub-contractor is legally bound to the requirements of the contract. The prime contractor will hold the sub-contractor liable with expectations to complete the scope of work.

When prime contractors are awarded contracts, to meet the requirements of the scope of work, they will need to hire sub-contractors. Also, it is important to know the FAR regulations regarding subcontracts. As stated in the FAR, prime contractors are mandated to award subcontracts to minority and women owned small businesses. It is recommended that you read the FAR regulations, outlined in part #44, on subcontracting and become familiar with the requirements and guidelines for subcontracting.

The definition for a subcontractor outlined in the FAR Part #44: "Subcontract" means any contract as defined in **Subpart 2.1** entered into by a subcontractor to furnish supplies or services for performance of a prime contract or a subcontract. It includes but is not limited to purchase orders, changes and modifications to purchase orders.

"Subcontractor" means any supplier, distributor, vendor, or firm that furnishes supplies or services to or for a prime contractor or another subcontractor. Companies enter into subcontracting arrangements for several reasons. They usually do not have the expertise in-house, and they need the services for a period that is not long enough to justify hiring a full-time person. For example, a residential construction company may hire subcontractors to complete the landscaping on houses, while the prime contractor on a defense project may hire subcontractors for writing technical manuals.

## Your Role As A Subcontractor

It may be a wise move for you to pursue subcontracting opportunities with prime contractors. Your role as a subcontractor could provide your company with the following benefits:

- ✓ Increases your capabilities and builds your business performance
- ✓ You do not have the responsibility for the entire contract and can still perform a portion of the scope of the work
- ✓ You have the opportunity to build your skills and learn from a company with experience

If you are thinking about subcontracting, you can visit the subnet portal to obtain a list of companies seeking subcontractors.

Table 1.1: Flow chart of your entry as a contractor in the federal marketplace:

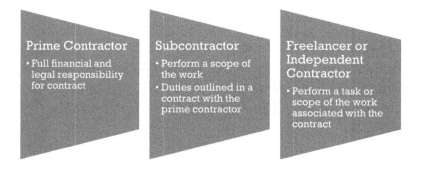

## Federal Compliance For Contractors

As a subcontractor, you are also required to comply with specific rules related to employment related activities. The Office of Federal Contract Compliance programs (OFCCP) is set up to ensure federal contractors and subcontractors provide fair employment opportunities and implement effective affirmative action steps with hiring practices. As a prime or subcontractor, it is extremely important for your business to stay in compliance to avoid adverse consequences. Here is a sample of the employment related areas that the agency focuses on:

- Hiring
- Promotions
- Recruitment
- Transfers
- Terminations

As you set up your compliance, be aware of the stipulations outlined in the following executive orders:

- Executive Order #11246
- Ssection 503 of the Rehabilitation Act
- Vietnam Era Veterans Readjustment Assistance Act (VEVRAA)

Here are some quick strategies that you should consider to be in compliance:

- Incorporate practices that do not discriminate based upon race, color, religion, sex or sexual orientation.
- Invest financially in a management software that will help you stay in compliance with your hiring, promotions and compensation decisions
- Maintain detailed records related to employee decisions for a minimum of two years
- Create an internal affirmative action program and keep updated annually
- Include a tagline that emphasizes that your company is an "Equal Opportunity Employer"

- Advertise your positions on diverse job boards
- Keep records on why you make hiring decisions
- Post Equal Opportunity Posters at various locations at your worksites

**Compliance Requirements: E-Verify**

E-Verify is a web-based system that confirms the eligibility of employees to work in the United States. Employers verify their identity and employment eligibility of newly hired employees by electronically matching information provided by employees on the Form I-9, Employment Eligibility Verification, against records available to the Social Security Administration (SSA) and the Department of Homeland Security (DHS). E-Verify is a voluntary program, however, employers with federal contracts or subcontracts are required to enroll in E-Verify as a condition of federal contracting. For additional information visit: **www.e-verify.com**

**Terminology And Acronyms**

The federal contracting process is a totally different from contracting in the private sector. The federal government is mandated by law to address small business concerns. As discussed in previous chapters, the federal government has programs, policies, rules and regulations that govern contracting and how you do business. The terminology is also different from the private sector. It is extremely important for you to take time and become familiar with terminology and what is required to be successful as a prime and subcontractor. Listed in the back section of the book is a list of acronyms that you should learn as a federal contractor.

# Chapter #4: Summary

- The FAR is a standardized set of regulations used by all federal agencies when they are making purchases. It provides procedures for every step of the procurement process, from the time that the government discovers a need for a product or service to the time the purchase is complete.

- Acquisition.gov is the online site to review "Agency Recurring Procurement Forecast" reports. Also, the 53 chapters of the FAR are listed on the website.

- There are laws and regulations that outline the federal contracting process.

- Prime contractors assume the full legal and financial responsibility for contracts, however, as a subcontractor, you are also required to be in compliance with human resources and accounting policies.

- The federal contracting process is a totally different from contracting in the private sector and other entities. The federal government is mandated by law to address small business concerns.

- You can pursue a federal contract as a prime or subcontractor. Subcontracting is an option to build your business experience and capability with contracting.

# CHAPTER #5
## CONTRACTING VEHICLES AND TRENDS

> This section provides you with an overview of the contracting vehicles utilized by the federal government to purchase goods and services. An important part of preparing your business to pursue contracting is studying the processes. If you understand how the government buys, you can posture your business for an opportunity with a process that does not require an extensive request for proposal submission. You can leverage contracting vehicles to possibly pursue a potential sole source or set aside contract opportunity as Women Owned Small Business. Study the contracting vehicles and the thresholds in this section thoroughly.

**Contracting Vehicles**

The Federal government utilizes standardized buying procedures to purchase goods and services from vendors/suppliers that is referred to as "contracting vehicles.". The rules and policies for each of the contracting vehicles are outlined in the Federal Acquisition Regulations (FAR). The following is a provides a brief overview of the contracting vehicles: Federal agencies are required to post purchases over $25,000 on the Federal Business Opportunities (FBO) website, the database for current procurement opportunities. However, as outlined in the Federal Acquisition Regulations (FAR), contracting officers are authorized to utilize the following contracting vehicles for purchases. This process reduces administrative costs, streamlines the process and provides the opportunity for women and small business purchases.

- **Credit Card/micro-purchases**
  Contracting officers can purchase items with a credit card as a micro

purchase. If the purchase is under $10,000, the bid or RFP process is not required.

- **Simplified Acquisition**
  A contracting officer can purchase goods and services under $250,000 using a simplified acquisition process. This process involves less paperwork and is also reserved or "set aside" exclusively for small businesses.

- **Sealed Bidding**
  A competitive process with specific requirements outlined in an Invitation to BID (IFB) or in a Request for Proposal (RFP). Contracts are awarded to the most responsive bidder

- **Contracts by Negotiations**
  A more complex process and time consuming and the value usually exceeds $150,000. It will usually require a technical product.

- **Consolidated Purchasing Vehicles** – Many agencies have common purchasing needs such as software or offices supplies.

## Leveraging Contracting Vehicles

As you pursue contract opportunities, you can leverage contracting vehicles for a potential opportunity. For

example, a Contracting Officer can purchase your goods or services with a credit card as a micro purchase. A micro credit card purchase under $10,000 does not require a bid or RFP process. Another example of a "no bid" opportunity is the simplified acquisition process. You can sell your products/services with a process that requires less paperwork. Both serve as great examples for small businesses to obtain contract opportunities from the federal government.

This was made possible as a result of the Federal Acquisition Streamlining Act, which removed competition restrictions on government purchases under $250,000. The **FAR Part #13** reduces administrative cost and increases opportunities for small, small disadvantaged, women-owned, veteran-owned, HUBZone, and service-disabled veteran-owned small business concerns.

**As outlined in FAR 13.106-2-13**.106-3, It clearly states that the contracting officer has broad discretion in fashioning suitable evaluation procedures. Meaning they can use their best interest to do the right thing for the good of the agency when conducting a simplified acquisition contract.

The Simplified Acquisition Program is a simple way to award contracts to small business owners. Procurement officers can award contracts without requiring the extensive paperwork required when submitting a Request for Proposal (RFP). Contracting officers can purchase lower cost items and not have to wait to receive proposals from interested suppliers/vendors. When contracting officers are purchasing goods and services via credit cards or through a simplified acquisition, the contracts are not posted online.

**Sole Source Contracts**

Another strategy for women owned businesses is to pursue a "sole source" contract. A "sole source" procurement is a contract that is awarded to a business entity without a competitive process. The decision to award a sole source

contract from a federal agency is usually based upon the following: only one known source exists or that only one single supplier can fulfill the requirements. As outlined in **FAR 13.106-1**, procurement officers can hire from one source immediately if that officer determines that the circumstance calls for it. The larger the contract, the more scrutiny it will be under. Large contracts above the simplified acquisition threshold must be documented in the Federal Awardee Performance and Integrity Information System (FAPIIS). Many contracting officers would rather award a Simplified Acquisition Contract simply to avoid the paperwork of (FAPIIS).

## Contracting Trends: Best In Class

Small Business Outreach events are a great resource to learn about future for federal contracting. At a recent conference, a GSA representative discussed in detail the trend for "Best in class". As stated on the GSA site, the best in class is described as follows:

**Best-in-Class (BIC)** means that something has been designated by the Office of Management and Budget (OMB) as a preferred government wide solution that:

- Allows acquisition experts to take advantage of pre-vetted, government
- Supports a government wide migration to solutions that are mature and market-proven
- Assists in the optimization of spend, within the government wide category management framework
- Increases the transactional data available for agency level and government wide analysis of buying behavior

This approach allows Federal agencies to make informed decisions with the sharing of information and data gathered as a result of agencies working together. It also allows the opportunity to reduce administrative cost and avoid contract duplication. The list below provides an overview of some of the categories described in the best in category:

- Transportation & Logistics
- Information Technology
- Professional Services
- Travel
- Medical
- Human Capital
- Office Management
- Facilities & Construction

- Industrial Products & Services
- Security & Protection

For additional information, go to gsa.gov and download the one page government wide category management BIC guide.

## Section #5: Chapter Summary

- The Federal government utilizes standardized buying procedures to purchase goods/services from vendors/suppliers.

- The rules and policies for each of the contracting vehicles are outlined in the Federal Acquisition Regulations (FAR).

- Contracting officers are authorized to utilize the following contracting vehicles for purchases: credit cards for micro purchases, simplified acquisitions, sealed bidding, contract by negotiation and consolidated purchasing vehicles.

- The Federal government post bid opportunities over $25,000 on the Fed Biz Opps online portal.

- Credit card micro purchases and simplified acquisitions are "no bid" contract opportunities for small business owners

- The Federal government post projected contract opportunities on acquisition.gov in the business zone area. You can review the Recurring Procurement Forecast" reports for federal agencies.

- **Best-in-Class (BIC)** designation is a preferred government wide solution that allows acquisition experts to take advantage of pre-vetted suppliers for common goods and services to avoid time and cost of conducting procurement.

# CHAPTER #6: ONLINE DATABASES

> The federal government has databases that provide you with an abundance of information related to past awards, quantities, costs and a listing of awardees. As you move forward, you can utilize the information to develop a marketing plan, study your competitors and understand how the government awards contracts.

**Listing of Government Databases**

The following databases are an invaluable source for researching current, past and future contracting opportunities.

- USA Spending
- Federal Register
- Fedbizopps
- Federal Procurement Data System (FPDS)
- Acquisition.gov
- Acquisition Gateway
- Dynamic Small Business Search (DSBS)
- Subnet Portal
- GSA elibrary

**USA Spending**

Federal agencies have financial budgets that are allocated for federal spending. Obligated amounts from federal spending are categorized in the form of grants, contracts, purchase orders and other instruments. This site provides a breakdown of spending for each federal agency. USA spending is also a great site to obtain specific geographical information regarding companies that are doing business in your area. If you want to get a quick snapshot of where the government is spending money, this is a great site. You can also search by your zip code to get a comprehensive listing of grants, contracts and loans.

**Tip: You can sign up to this site to receive updates about spending with the federal government**

Site Screenshot:

**USA spending.gov**

**Federal Register**
Want to stay on top with things that go on with the federal government. There are constantly notices and information that is changing. This is an invaluable site, you can track notices and information about new rulings, etc. The Federal register is the official journal of the federal government of the United States. The site contains rules and public notices and the information is published daily except for holidays. Here is a list of what is published:

- Proposed new rules and regulations
- Final rules
- Changes to existing rules
- Notices of meetings and proceedings

- Presidential documents including Executive orders, proclamations and administrative orders.

Site Screenshot:

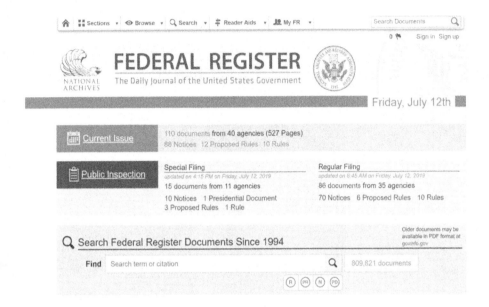

www.federalregister .com

## FED Biz Opps

Fed Biz Opps is a great site for monitoring potential contracts and sources sought notices. This site is also filled with valuable information regarding opportunities, agencies and training. If you are ready to pursue contracts, you can search for open opportunities. However, you can still utilize this site for other critical information. You can set up a profile with a password for entry and get notified of contract opportunities by checking the advanced search boxes.

Click on the "Getting Started" tab for the following instructions:

- General Overview and how to search for opportunities
- Instructions to register and login
- How to use advanced functionality, search agents & watch lists

Site Screenshot:

**Fedbizopps.**
Guess What! Sources Sought notices are posted on Fedbizopps. Gov. Although a Sources Sought notice is not an actual RFP, you can still respond and begin building a relationship with a contracting officer. Responding to the notice is a great way to get started with federal contracting.

**Federal Procurement Data System**

FPDS is an invaluable site to research companies that have secured federal contracts. You can create an account that allows you to log in with your password. It is advisable to create a login account, if you would like to utilize the site to create customized or Adhoc reports.

Site Screenshot:

**Fpds.gov**
However, you can utilize the EZSearch function to quickly review information about companies without creating an account. In the EZsearch area, place the name of the company in the search box.

1) If the company has a current or past contract with the federal government, their name will appear and a box will pop up that will list their past or current contracts.
2) You can navigate to the far right column and click on (date signed) to get a listing of the most recent contract.
3) You can acquire additional detailed contract information by clicking on the (View) button. This site also contains reports and other information.

**Acquisition GOV**
Acquisition.gov contains information regarding potential projected upcoming

procurement opportunities with the federal government. Search this database for projected procurement reports by agencies.

Site Screenshot:

**www.acquisition.gov**

Here are the instructions to review the procurement forecasting reports:

1) Go to Acquisition.gov
2) Scroll down to the Business Zone
3) Under the Business Zone Section
4) Click on Agency Recurring Forecasts
5) In the Agency Procurement Forecasts click on Procurement Forecasts
6) A listing of federal agencies will populate
7) Highlight the agency of your interest

This is the location to review forecast reports listed by federal agencies. Please note, the formats will be different for each agency. Additionally, not all of the agencies keep their list updated. Utilize this site as a great resource of information regarding projected opportunities.

The Following listing of federal agencies will appear:

Department of Agriculture
Department of Commerce
Department of Education
Department of Energy
Department of Justice
Department of Labor
Department of State
Department of Veterans Affairs
Department of Housing and Urban Development
General Services Administration
Office of Personnel Management
Social Security Administration

Click on any of the agencies and you can review a projected procurement forecast report for the agency.

**Acquisition Gateway**

A valuable online website for contractors is acquisition gateway, an online portal built by General Services Administration (GSA). Acquisition Gateway is a workspace for acquisition professionals and federal buyers to connect with resources, tools, and acquisition government-wide acquisition information.

Site Screenshot:

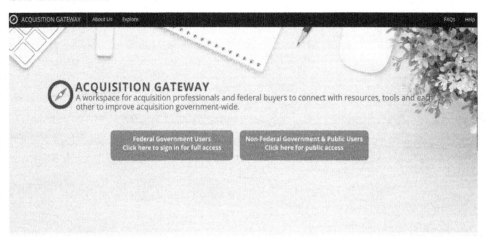

**Hallways.cap.gsa.gov**

The site is a valuable resource for the following information:

- View government-wide contracts and solutions.
- Connect with other acquisition professionals and Contracting Officers
- Explore product and service category
- Find articles, statement of work (SOW) samples, acquisition templates, market research tools, prices paid data and best practices

There is certain information that is only available to government employees. However, the general public has access to a majority of the information on the gateway. Users of the system have to read and review the privacy statement.

## Dynamic Small Business Search

The Small Business Administration (SBA) maintains the Dynamic Small Business Search (DSBS) database. When you register your business in the System for Award Management (SAM), there is an opportunity to fill out the small business profile. The information that you input into the SAM will populate into the DSBS.

# Site Screenshot: Dynamic Small Business Search

https://web.sba.gov/pro-net/search/dsp_dsbs.cfm

DSBS database is another tool contracting officers use to identify potential small business contractors for upcoming contracting opportunities. This is also a great site to obtain information about your potential competitors and other companies. You can search by a range of variables which includes socioeconomic status, number of employees and NAICS codes.

## Subnet Portal

The Small Business Administration (SBA) encourages prime contractors and subcontractors to reach out to small business
owners by posting their opportunities on this site. SUB-Net
has been used by state/local governments, non-profit organizations, colleges and universities to post solicitations and identify small businesses. The subnet portal is a great site to start your search for potential opportunities. Although the SBA provides the directory, it does not have the authority to require a prime contractor to utilize your business.

Site Screenshot:

**www.subnetportal**

To find subcontracting opportunities, go to SUB-Net, SBA's database, where you will be able to review the site to identify subcontracting opportunities that align with your area of expertise. It's easy to search all solicitations or simply search by NAICS Code for a listing of subcontracting opportunities. The subnet site contains the name of the company, the closing date and a detailed description of subcontracting opportunities available. This is a great site to visit to obtain a summary of possible subcontracting opportunities. However, the site does not contain information for all of the federal contractors that may have possible sub-contracts. Therefore, you should utilize several databases and conduct intensive research to identify opportunities.

**Summary: Databases**

The chart below illustrates the information that is in each of the online databases operated by the federal government.

| Data Base | Information |
|---|---|
| **USA Spending.gov** | A spending map of the dollars spent by the federal government. You can search for a listing of the contracts, grants and loans by city, zip codes and other variables. You can also search for a listing of companies that are doing business in your area. |
| **Federal Register** | The official journal for the US Federal government contains agency rules and public notices. |
| **FedBizOpps** | This database contains a listing of federal business opportunities, solicitations and current RFP's. You can create a log in and password and get notified of projected contract opportunities. |
| **Federal Procurement Data System Fpds.gov** | A great resource to research companies that were awarded contracts with the federal government. You can do an EZ search to get a quick glimpse of companies and information regarding past and current federal contracts. |
| **Acquisition.gov** | You can view the FAR, search by agency name and get a list of projected procurement opportunities. There are also useful resource links for training information, and OSDBU officers. |
| **Subnet.gov** | A site for prime contractors to post subcontracting opportunities |
| **Acquisition Gateway** | Acquisition Gateway is a workspace for acquisition professionals and federal buyers to connect with resources, tools, and acquisition government-wide acquisition information. |

| | |
|---|---|
| **Dynamic Small Business Search (DSBS)** | A self-certification Database that can be searched with the following variables: state, government certifications, ownership, NAICS codes, size and profiles. |
| **GSA elibrary** | GSA contract award information Searchable database, keywords, schedule, NAICS codes List of participating vendors Technical proposals Pricing information and job descriptions |

**Chapter #6: Summary**

- The government is transparent, and the online databases contains pertinent information related to past, current and upcoming contracts/opportunities.

- Utilize databases to gather information that will be included in your contraction plan of actin (CPA).

- Stay informed and visit the FAR website to review policies and practices related to contracting.

- Track federal government spending habits with USA Spending to see who is doing business in your area, and the flow of contracts, loans, etc.

- Utilize the databases to compile information that you can include as you prospect for potential prime and subcontract opportunities.

- The databases can be utilized to research companies receiving prime contracts from the federal government.

- Visit the SBA subnet portal to research and review subcontracting plans for private companies receiving large prime contracts.

- Visit FPDS.gov to research potential companies and review contract information.

- Research GSA elibrary to obtain a listing of companies doing business with federal agencies that match your NAICS codes to get an idea of the agencies buying your goods and services.

# CHAPTER #7: FEDERAL GRANTS

> The government provides grants for entities that are "for profit" in specialized areas which includes research and development. However, it is unlikely that grants are available to launch a business idea. Take time and visit the sites that we discuss in this section to explore the viability of a grant opportunity for your business. Do your research!

**Federal Grants For Business Owners**

We often see numerous advertisements and books stating that you could receive grants and free money for your business from the federal government. Several years ago there was a book written about all the free government money available to individuals and grants for businesses. To this date, federal agencies still receive calls from entrepreneurs asking about grants for their small businesses.

Finding FREE money in the form of a grant is like searching for a needle in a haystack. As an entrepreneur, it would be great to secure a grant that would provide me with resources for a business enterprise. Grants are usually awarded to nonprofit organizations that have the 50lc3 designation from the Internal Revenue Service (IRS). This designation allows a tax deduction for donations made to qualified nonprofit organizations and charities. Government grants are rarely available for business owners for several reasons. Government grants are funded with your tax dollars and there are specific rules on how the funds are utilized. However, grants are available to businesses within specific industries that are involved in research and development. The federal government provides grants to small businesses that are engaged in scientific research under the Small Business Innovation Research Program (SBIR) monitored by the Small Business Administration (SBA). The Following is an overview of the special programs:

# Special Grant Programs

## The America's Seed Fund

The America's Seed Fund under the National Science Foundation (NSF) provides financial support to help small businesses and startups transform their ideas into marketable services and products. The overall goal of the agency is to foster innovation and help create businesses and jobs in America.

Site Screenshot:

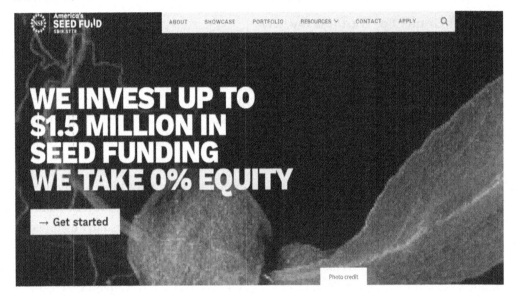

**seedfund.nsf.gov**

The program provides the following:

- Seed capital for early stage product development for early stage research and development.
- Access to a network of innovators and industry experts
- Access to a diverse portfolio of funded startups and small businesses across technology areas and markets.

# The SBIR Program

The Small Business Innovation Research (SBIR) program is a highly competitive program that encourages domestic small businesses to engage in Federal Research/Research and Development (R/R&D) that has the potential for commercialization. Through a competitive awards-based program, SBIR enables small businesses to explore their technological potential and provides the incentive to profit from its commercialization.

Site Screenshot:

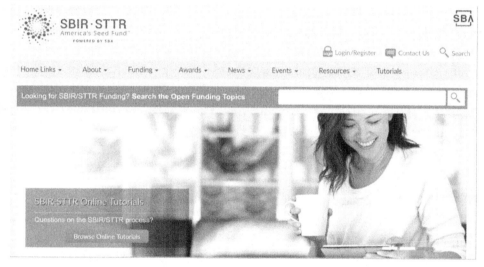

www.sbir.gov

# The STTR Program

The Small Business Technology Transfer (STTR) is another program that expands funding opportunities in the federal innovation research and development (R&D) arena. Central to the program is expansion of the public/private sector partnership to include the joint venture opportunities for small businesses and non-profit research institutions.

## The STTR Program

*The following information is cited from the STTR website:*

The Small Business Technology Transfer (STTR) is a program that expands funding opportunities in the federal innovation research and development (R&D) arena. Central to the program is expansion of the public/private sector partnership to include the joint venture opportunities for small businesses and nonprofit research institutions. The unique feature of the STTR program is the requirement for the small business to formally collaborate with a research institution in Phase I and Phase II. STTR supports scientific excellence and technological innovation through the investment of Federal research funds in critical American priorities to build a strong national economy. Each year, Federal agencies with extramural research and development (R&D) budgets that exceed $1 billion are required to reserve 0.45% of the extramural research budget for STTR awards to small businesses. These agencies designate R&D topics and accept proposals. Currently, five agencies participate in the STTR program:

- Department of Defense
- Department of Energy
- Department of Health and Human Services
- National Aeronautics and Space Administration
- National Science Foundation

Each agency administers its own individual program within guidelines established by Congress. These agencies designate R&D topics in their solicitations and accept proposals from small businesses. Awards are made on a competitive basis after proposal evaluation.

Visit the site to obtain additional information that includes the following:

- Application timelines

- How to prepare a proposal
- Funding information
- Listing of awards
- Events and Webinars
- External Resources
- FAQ Links

**Grant for Business and Non-Profits**

If you have a non-profit agency with the 501(C) 3 IRS designations, you can definitely qualify for grants or pursue a contract from the federal government. An invaluable website is grants.gov., a comprehensive database of federal funding opportunities.

Site Screenshot:

**www.grants.gov**

This site contains a wealth of information about grants and instructional videos on every topic providing an opportunity to learn on-line about how to apply for grants with the federal government. You can also do a basic search to get a list of current federal funding opportunities. When you visit grants.gov, go to the eligibility category that is located on the far right column and navigate to the eligibility section (see example of information on the site below). The following is a snapshot of the categories listed on the site:

Opportunity Status:
- Forecasted
- Posted
- Closed
- Archived
- 

Funding Instrument type
- Cooperative Agreement
- Grant
- Other
- Procurement

Other searchable categories include:
- Eligibility
- Category
- Agencies

The grants.gov site has a great learning center filled with searchable resources – here is a screenshot of the learning center:

Located on grants.gov is a great "Grant Learning Center" that provides a range of information on the following topics:

- Grant policies and eligibility
- Programs
- Grant Reporting
- Uniform Administrative Requirements

The grants.gov is an online site that is an online destination to obtain information for grant programs offered by Federal agencies. The office of Management and Budget (OMB) requires federal agencies to post their grant applications directly to grants.gov. The site also allows organizations and businesses to electronically find and apply for competitive grant opportunities. You can search and electronically submit your proposals through the grants.gov portal and they will be forwarded electronically to the respective funding agency.

Another useful site for resources is usa.gov. The site contains a host of information related to programs and information for federal, state and local governments.

**Site Screenshot usa.gov**

# Chapter #7: SUMMARY

- Grants are available to businesses within specific industries that are involved in research and development.

- The federal government provides grants to small businesses that are engaged in scientific research under the Small

- The Small Business Innovation Research (SBIR) program is a highly competitive program that encourages domestic small businesses to engage in Federal Research/Research and Development (R/R&D) that has the potential for commercialization.

- The Small Business Technology Transfer (STTR) is a program that expands funding opportunities in the federal innovation research and development (R&D) arena.

- An invaluable website is grants.gov. The grants.gov site provides detailed information on applying for a grant and also publishes upcoming grant opportunities. The site also allows organizations and businesses to electronically find and apply for competitive grant opportunities.

- The office of Management and Budget (OMB) requires federal agencies to post their grant applications directly to grants.gov.

# CHAPTER #8: SUPPLIER DIVERSITY

> Supplier Diversity is another program that is beneficial for women in business. Supplier diversity programs are initiatives that support and promotes the participation of women and minority business enterprises. If you are interested in doing business with a corporation or company, it may work to your advantage to take a moment and visit their website and review their supplier diversity policies.

**Overview of Supplier Diversity**

During the previous chapters, we focused our discussion on the process for doing business with the federal government. We will now switch to doing business with corporations and other entities. Let's begin with a discussion of "Supplier Diversity". Supplier Diversity is a business strategy that encourages companies to utilize small and diverse women and minority owned businesses in the contracting process. Supplier diversity programs encourage the procurement of goods and services from small and diverse owned businesses. When we discuss federal contracting, we refer to women owned small businesses programs. Supplier Diversity is a term that is utilized by corporations and companies in the private sector.

**Why Supplier Diversity**

From a business perspective, it makes sense to have diversity programs that reflect the community and business customers. Corporations and companies utilizing "supplier Diversity programs" as a strategy to reach minority and women owned businesses. The following outlines the objectives of supplier diversity initiatives:

- Promotes innovation with opportunities for new companies to showcase products, solutions and services
- Demonstrates the company's commitment to doing business with a diverse group of suppliers that represents the community

- Promotes competition with existing and prospective vendors
- Provides a wider choice and options to purchase goods and services
- Demonstrates that the company has an interest in job creation and the economic growth of the community
- Confirms the commitment of the company to doing business with a diverse group of suppliers/vendors

Overall, supplier diversity is beneficial and is a driving economic force for the growth of diverse businesses. As small businesses grow, so will the nation's economy. Since most diverse businesses are small businesses, they aid in the economic recovery and sustainability of communities. In addition, supplier diversity is important because it provides products and services to emerging consumer markets. While traditional products and services remain available to consumers, demographic shifts create opportunities for diverse suppliers to meet the needs of emerging and/or shifting populations in the U.S. and on a global level.

## Do You Qualify As A Diverse Supplier

In prior chapters, we discussed women owned small business programs available as part of the federal contracting process. On the other hand, supplier diversity programs are designed to promote the inclusion and participation of women owned and minority businesses with the private sector market. Corporations and private companies utilize Supplier diversity programs as a strategy that encourages women and minority owned businesses to participate in the procurement process. The term "Diverse Supplier" is important for supplier diversity programs. A diverse supplier is an entrepreneur or a business entity that is at least 51% owned, operated and controlled by a person of a diverse background (minority, woman, Lesbian, Gay, Bisexual Transgender (LGBT), Veteran owned or a Disabled Veteran.

If your business meets one or more of the following criteria's, then you are a diverse supplier:

- Minority Owned Business Enterprise (MOBE)
- Women Owned Small Business (WOSB)
- Women Business Enterprise (WBE)
- Veteran
- Disabled Service Veteran (DV)

A major corporation will have thousands of suppliers/vendors providing a wide range of products and services to multiple geographic areas. Remember, the corporate sector is different from the federal sector and you need to understand the following terminology:

- **Tier 1:** Prime Supplier responsible for the contract and will submit invoices directly to the corporate customer. Due to established relationships, procurement opportunities are managed by major prime contractors or business partners.
- **Tier 2**: Subcontractor reports to the Prime Contractor (tier 1) and is only responsible for a scope of work under the Prime contractor.

Request for payments and invoices will be submitted directly to the Prime Contractor. The subcontractor will not have a relationship with the Company.

## Your Strategy

You can utilize supplier diversity programs as a way to get noticed by a company and let them know that you exist. Additionally, you learned from previous chapters that prime contractors receiving large federal contracts are mandated to develop subcontracting plans that target small business participation. Federal contracts are awarded to corporations and private companies. The Federal Procurement Database System (FPDS) is a great site to review government contracts awarded to companies. You can do an easy search by company name and the site will populate contract information. For example, information posted in the Federal Procurement Database stated that Accenture was awarded a five-year contract worth $17.9 million to upgrade the U.S. Securities and Exchange Commission platform awarded to Accenture. The company was also awarded a two-year management consulting contract from the Office of the National Coordinator for Health Information Technology, a division within the U.S. Department of Health and Human Services.

Possibly, this could be a great opportunity for you to receive a subcontract to perform a scope of the work. If your NAICS codes match the work outlined in the contract and you are interested in doing business, you should visit Accenture's website and process for registering as a supplier on their Supplier Connection Page. This is one example of a company that does business with the federal government. *Could this be an opportunity for you to get a piece of the pie?*

**Case Studies: Supplier Diversity**

Conducting research is an extremely important step to identify potential companies that can eventually be your customer. This is a step that we call "prospecting", which requires you to obtain detailed information that includes tracking previous contracts, what type of services/products are purchased and their supplier diversity policies. Let's closely examine information from four companies that have supplier diversity initiatives.

Here is the list:
1. Georgia Power
2. Walmart
3. Coca-Cola Company
4. JE Dunn

**GEORGIA POWER – SOUTHERN COMPANY**

The following Statement is on the Georgia Power website at:

www.georgiapower.com:

At Southern Company, we take great pride in developing strong, long-term and trusting relationships with suppliers that will help drive value for our company and our customers. Our customer base of more than 9 million customers is quite diverse. Our mission is to reflect that diversity in the suppliers that help energize our success. Southern Company and its subsidiaries are committed to supply chain diversity across the Southeast.

*With a corporate focus on maintaining the diversity of our suppliers, Georgia Power and Southern Company have designed award-winning initiatives to provide solid business opportunities for small and diverse businesses. These include the following categories:*

- *Minority-owned*
- *HUBZone*
- *Veteran-owned small*
- *Service disabled veteran-owned small*
- *Woman-owned small*
- *Small disadvantaged business concerns*

*The company values are illustrated on the next table:*

## Demonstrated Commitment

 Build awareness around our Company's commitment to a diversified supply chain.

 Comply with all requirements, guidelines, and procedures of regulatory agencies.

 Hold ourselves accountable through aggressive performance standards.

 Administer effective processes for measuring and reporting diverse spend performance both externally and internally.

 Leverage diversity when evaluating sourcing opportunities.

## Collaborative Engagement

 Engage with our internal business partners by recruiting quality, reliable, competitive diverse suppliers who can meet or exceed their operational needs.

 Create an inclusive environment across stakeholder groups that capitalizes on the value of business diversity.

 Seek suppliers who can provide our business units with innovative, cost effective solutions to emerging challenges.

After reviewing their website, it states that the company is interested in doing business with a small and diverse group of business owners. It is important for you to take time and thoroughly review the information posted on the website of the companies that you are seeking to pursue for business. Reach out to the contact person and start building a relationship.

*As a small business owner, you may also benefit from one of the following Southern Company programs that support growing businesses:*

### Southern Company helps growing businesses

**Mentor Program**
Our Mentor Program helps build relationships between Southern Company employees with buying authority and minority and female suppliers, enabling suppliers to increase awareness of opportunities at Southern Company, and giving purchasing employees wider supplier choices.

**Minority Business Executive Program**
We provide sponsorships for qualified, proven suppliers to attend Dartmouth University's Tuck School of Business, where they attend classes that focus on building high-performing businesses.

**Second Tier Program**
Southern Company strongly encourages prime suppliers to extend subcontracting opportunities to minority-owned and female-owned firms. This program has added opportunities for minority businesses in companies we do not own or manage.

*Please note:*
*There are requirements and a selection process for all these programs. If you'd like to get more information, please send an e-mail to supplierdiv@southernco.com.*

## WALMART

The following statement is on Walmart's website:

"As the world's largest retailer, Walmart strives to save people money so they can live better. This mantra is at the core of every decision we make. One way we fulfill this commitment is to embrace diversity in all aspects of our organization; from our talented associates to the supplier partners we work with to deliver the products and services our customers want and need."

Go to Walmart's Supplier Inclusion page and navigate to the section title "Become a Diverse Supplier". On the page you can to to "FAQs" and click on the question "What are the certification agencies recognized by Walmart." The following is a list of certifications that are recognized by Walmart (source: Walmart.com/supplier diversity).

- U.S. Business Leadership Network (USBLN)
- U.S. Pan Asian American Chamber of Commerce (USPAACC)
- Federal government
- Local government
- DD Form 214
- WE Connect International
- Department of Veterans Affairs Center for Veterans Enterprises

As demonstrated from the list, Walmart will recognize certifications from the federal government and other local government entities. Therefore, if you get certified by the Small Business Administration (SBA), Walmart will acknowledge the certifications from the Small Business Administration (SBA).

**COCA-COLA COMPANY**

Another popular company that women and minorities seek to do business with is The Coca-Cola. The following is a statement the appears on the supplier diversity page:

*The Coca-Cola Company is committed to supplier diversity by maximizing procurement opportunities and proactively engaging and building partnerships with diverse suppliers. Supplier diversity is an integral component of the Company's diversity management strategy and we believe that including our customers and consumers in our procurement strategy will help develop stronger local communities and create long-term growth and a competitive advantage for the Coca-Cola system.*

Coca-Cola also has other initiatives under their supplier diversity program listed as a resource on the company website. There is a program that connects business partners with prime suppliers and business development training. If you are interested in being a supplier, you are encouraged to visit the Coca Cola supplier diversity website and register your business. The following is a listing of the certifications that the company will acknowledge:

- Small Business Administration SBA - 8(a) or Small Disadvantaged Business (SDB) Programs
- US Pan Asian Chamber of Commerce (USPAACC)
- Women's Business Enterprise National Council (WBENC)
- National Women's Business Owners Corporation (NWBOC)
- The National Gay and Lesbian Chamber of Commerce (NGLCC)
- US Department of Veteran Affairs (VA)
- Source: **www.coca-cola.com**

The Coca-Cola Company will accept certifications from The Small Business Administration as well as third party certifiers. If you are a new business, you can start with the certifications offered by the Small Business Administration (SBA).

# JE DUNN CONSTRUCTION

JE Dunn Construction is another company that with supplier diversity programs and initiatives.

### As stated in JE Dunn's literature:

*JE Dunn has a long-standing commitment to help minority and women-owned business enterprises succeed. JE Dunn's Minority Contractor's Business Development (MCBD) program focuses on building the business and leadership skills necessary for companies to compete in the construction industry. The unique program covers the following topics: bidding, competing, project leadership, Human resources, time management and scheduling. Your participation in the MCBD program will provide you with critical skills that will support your success. Visit JE Dunn's website for additional information and reach out to the supplier diversity professionals.*

Site Screenshot:

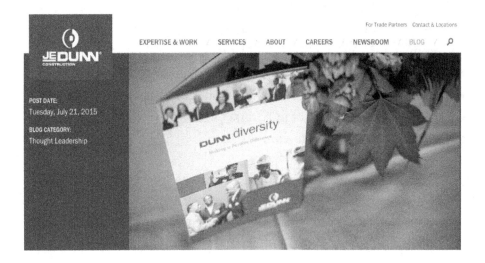

## Case Studies: Learning Tips

After a review of the case studies, you should learn the following:

- The Georgia Power company is an award-winning agency with a commitment to diverse suppliers. The website does not list any certification preferences or requirements. Therefore, the first steps would be to register in the portal as a vendor and reach out to the Supplier Diversity Division to have a further conversation. This is a great opportunity to begin building a relationship that could possibly create a contract opportunity.

- Wal-Mart recognizes certifications from several entities, which include federal and local government. If you certify with the Small Business Administration (SBA) as a Women Owned Small Business (WOSB) or as an Economically Disadvantaged Owned Small Business (EDWOSB), these certifications would be acceptable.

- Coca-Cola also recognizes certification from the Small Business Administration (SBA) as an 8(a) Small Disadvantaged Business (SDB) and from the U.S. Department of Veterans Affairs.

- JE Dunn's has a specialized program that is targeted for women and minority owned companies interested in pursuing contracting opportunities in the construction industry.

Overall, to do business with any of the four companies listed, you can obtain a FREE certification status from the U.S. Small Administration (SBA) qualifying you to secure contracts with corporations. Remember to do your research and study the websites for any company that you are seeking to pursue contract opportunities. Visit the following website for detailed information regarding self-certifications: **www.certify.sba.gov.**

Supplier diversity programs can provide you with an opportunity to promote your business, however, you still have to be prepared. When you approach a corporation, you should be prepared to do business and present a professional image of your company. For example, you should have professional business cards, website presence and marketing materials. Supplier Diversity programs can help you get noticed, however, the opportunities are competitive and there are no set aside programs for women or minorities.

There is a difference between Federal programs and Supplier Diversity initiatives. As discussed in previous chapters, the federal government is mandated by policies and legislations to address small business concerns and reach business goals. In the private sector, companies make "good faith" efforts to promote diversity within their procurement processes. There are no guarantees for business opportunities.

The good news is that some corporations are now recognizing federal certifications. Take time to conduct research and visit the websites for the companies you are seeking to target for business opportunities. For example, if you visit **Target's supplier diversity** page it will outline their commitment to supplier diversity and include a listing of business classifications.

Overall, Supplier diversity is beneficial to all stakeholders, not just to the companies with programs. First and foremost, supplier diversity programming is a driving economic force for the growth of diverse businesses. As small businesses grow, so will our nation's economy. Since most diverse businesses are small businesses, they aid in the economic recovery and sustainability of their communities. In addition, supplier diversity is important because it provides products and services to emerging consumer markets. While traditional products and services remain available to consumers, demographic shifts create opportunities for diverse suppliers to meet the needs of emerging and/or shifting populations in the U.S. and across the globe.

# Chapter #8: Summary

- Supplier Diversity is a business strategy that encourages companies to utilize small and diverse women and minority owned businesses in the contracting process. Supplier diversity programs encourage the procurement of goods and services from small and diverse owned businesses.

- Diversity programs reflect the community and business customers. Corporations and companies utilize "supplier Diversity programs" as a strategy to reach minority and women owned businesses.

- Research and visit the websites of the companies that could be potential customers. Review contracting policies and certification requirements listed on company websites.

- Follow the registration procedures and get registered in portals to receive updated listings of potential contract opportunities.

- It is important to conduct research and approach companies that are purchasing your goods and services. Prior to making an approach, prepare professional marketing materials and presentations.

- When you make your approach, be specific about your request and do not approach companies that are not purchasing your goods or services

# CHAPTER # 9: CONTRACT READY

> In the previous chapters, we discussed federal contracting, supplier diversity programs and strategies for securing contracts. This chapter will focus on the preparation required to be contract ready. You are competing with hundreds of other businesses and you should prepare, plan and set your business up for success!

**Contract Ready Checklist**

Are you contract ready, and if you are not it takes time and preparation to pursue contracts with the federal government or any business sector. Here are a few contact ready questions that you should consider as you pursue contracts/business opportunities:

1. Are you legally set up to do business?
2. Are registered in the System for Award Management (SAM)?
3. Do You know your NAICS codes?
4. Are you certified as a WOSB?
5. Are you prepared financially if you were awarded a prime contract?
6. Are you familiar with the all the certification processes for the Small Business Administration (SBA)?
7. Do you have a capability statement?
8. Do you have business plan?
9. Do you have a website with a business email address?
10. What are your business strengths?
11. Do you have past performance within the industry?
12. Can you provide a quality product/service to the prime contractor?
13. Can you meet all the deadlines outlined in the RFP or contract?
14. Do you have the staff, resources and support to successfully complete the contract requirements?
15. Do you have the financial resources to support staff, or subcontractors required to successfully complete the contract?

## Contracting Strategies

When you pursue contract opportunities in the federal or private sector, you have options. If you are going to pursue an opportunity as a prime contractor, you and your team should have the technical expertise and capabilities to respond to a bid or a Request for Proposal (RFP). Review the request thoroughly and pay close attention to the time frames, scope of work, financial responsibilities, limits and restrictions.

If you are not prepared to assume a prime contract, subcontracting may be an option for you. Subcontractors work for the prime contractors on major projects or for companies that need specific tasks completed in a limited timeframe. Companies enter into subcontracting arrangements to complete a portion or scope of the work. If you need to build past performance, it may be a good idea to pursue work as a subcontractor for the following reasons:

- ✓ Build your performance and business capabilities
- ✓ You do not have the sole financial responsibility for the contract
- ✓ You have the opportunity to learn from a company with experience
- ✓ You can acquire the knowledge and expertise to become a prime contractor

As stated in the previous chapters, if you are doing business with the federal government or any entity, you need to complete all the registration processes required for the entity that you are seeking business contracts.

## Contracting Options: Teaming And Joint Ventures

Forming partnerships and joint ventures is another strategy for securing large prime contract opportunities. If you see an opportunity and want to pursue it, it could make sense to partner with a company that can provide the valuable skills and experience to help you win a contract. Perhaps you can consider collaboration as an option to pursue a contract. The opportunity to pursue a business opportunity with another small business owner can help you save costs and increase your options for adding expertise. Before you take the leap, carefully evaluate the legalities of partnering with another company and how it may impact the contract.

If you are pursuing federal contract opportunities, teaming arrangements are an excellent strategy. Teaming with another business provides you with an opportunity to combine your resources with another company. The following is a listing of benefits and considerations for creating a teaming arrangement with another company:

- Share risks and cost associated with contracts
- Collaborate on contracts and short-term projects
- Build your business capability and performance
- Access to additional resources and technical expertise
- Increase your capacity to bid on larger projects

Before you take the leap, it is important for you to select a business that closely aligns with your core business values and will display trust and integrity when conducting business.

**Teaming And Federal Contracts**

As I stated in previous chapters, it is important for you to plan, prepare and be strategic about your business decisions. The decision to partner or team with another company is a big move. I encourage my students to become familiar with the Federal Acquisition Regulations (FAR). This is what we refer to as the bible for Federal contracting. Utilize the information contained in the FAR as a point of reference. For example, if you are considering teaming with another company to pursue a federal contract, **review information contained in FAR 9.6** on teaming.

Here is a review of what is outlined in the section:

**FAR: 9.601** Definition.

Contractor team arrangement, refer to the following:
(1) Two or more companies form a partnership or joint venture to act as a potential prime contractor; or
(2) A potential prime contractor agrees with one or more other companies to have them act as its subcontractors under a specified Government contract or acquisition program.

**FAR: 9.602** General.

Contractor team arrangements may be desirable from both a Government and industry standpoint to enable the companies involved to:
(1) Complement each other's unique capabilities; and
(2) Offer the Government the best combination of performance, cost, and delivery for the system or product being acquired.
(b) Contractor team arrangements may be particularly appropriate in complex research and development acquisitions, but may be used in other appropriate acquisitions, including production.
(c) The companies involved normally form a contractor team arrangement before submitting an offer. However, they may enter into an arrangement later in the acquisition process, including after the contract award.

The Government will recognize the integrity and validity of contractor team arrangements; PROVIDED, the arrangements are identified, and company relationships are fully disclosed in an offer or, for arrangements entered into after submission of an offer, before the arrangement becomes effective. The Government will not normally require or encourage the dissolution of contractor team arrangements.

# CONTRACTING OPTIONS

You should know that when prime contractors are awarded contracts, in order to meet the requirements of the scope of work, they will need to hire sub-contractors. Although you may not be ready to pursue an opportunity as a Prime Contractor, there are other options you may want to consider. The table below outlines some additional options for your contracting strategy:

| TYPE | DEFINITION | BENEFITS |
|---|---|---|
| Prime Contractor (Full Responsibility) | Local, federal and state contracts provide a contract opportunity to one entity. The Prime contractor has the sole responsibility to meet the contract requirements and scope of work. | The prime has the full control and responsibility for meeting the contract requirements. |
| Subcontractor (Perform scope of work) | Working with a large prime contractor to complete a portion of the work. | Operating as a subcontractor provides the opportunity for your company to build capabilities expertise; and learn from a prime contractor. |
| Teaming Arrangement (Working with other companies) | Two or more companies join forces to pursue a government contract. One company will serve as the Prime Contractor and is responsible for the contract requirements. Other companies/ contractors agree to team and sign a teaming agreement with the prime. | The arrangement offers the government a combination of skills and expertise of each company. The companies form a contractor agreement before the bid is submitted. Companies involved will build skills and capabilities as a government contractor. |
| Joint Venture | A partnership with two or more Companies/ Contractors to collective pursue a procurement opportunity as a Prime Contractor. | The JV partners complete a "Contractor Team Arrangement Application." This allows the opportunity to pursue larger contracts with the combined expertise as a result of the JV. The SBA has the authority to review terms of the JV agreement. |

> **STRATEGY TIP**
> *It may be wise for you to consult with an attorney before signing a Teaming or Joint Venture agreement for the following considerations: termination of contract, sharing costs, licensing of intellectual property and affiliated relationships.*

If you are considering teaming or doing a joint venture with another company, the following is a list of considerations:

- The credit rating of the business

- Previous business references and relationships
- The financial capability of the business
- The business reputation of the business
- The expertise of the management and staff
- Is the company financially stable to assume obligations related to the performance of the contract

Basically, teaming arrangements are beneficial for you and for the federal government. Companies can join efforts and complement their unique capabilities.

Before you take the leap, make sure you do your research and carefully evaluate the benefits of entering into a teaming arrangement with another company. Think about this arrangement like you would your marriage, you are taking on a critical partner that could be a vital part of your business.

**Scope of Work Document**

An important part of doing business is writing a scope of work (SOW), especially for sub and independent contractors. You have probably heard the phrase "get it in writing" and this is very important for an entrepreneur or small business owner. A scope of work is a formal written document that outlines specifically the work activities, deliverables and timelines involved with a project. A Scope of Work document is sometimes referred to as a "statement of work" and can be used to describe the work plan.

The following is a sample of the industries that utilize a scope of work:
- Construction
- Marketing
- Event Planners
- Web/graphic design
- Software Development

## Scope of Work: Case Example

Here is a case example of why a scope of work is critical: AXZ is a prime contractor and during a casual conversation over lunch, he informed you that

his company was in need of an expert with software management experience. AXY Company was just awarded a major contract from the Federal government. Mr. Jones, a representative with the company asked you how much you would charge to provide a specific scope of work. During a casual conversation over lunch, you responded with the price of $75.00 per hour. He said great, can you start on Monday and just come to our office.

When you arrived back to your office, you received an email from Mr. Jones that outlined what work was necessary for the project. Upon careful review, you discovered that the scope of work was more detailed, and you would also have to secure additional team members to complete the work. After a few calculations, you discovered that you underestimated the hourly wage because the technical expertise required for the subcontract was higher than you estimated.

There were a few things that you did wrong with this negotiation. First, before you give a price, it is important for you to examine and have a thorough discussion what the scope of work would involve. A scope of work will protect you and help you formulate a fair and equitable price for your work. You need to have an in-depth conversation with Mr. Jones about what would be involved with the work. The lesson learned from this example is to give careful consideration to the following before you give a quote:

- Expenses related to indirect costs
- Overall work activities
- Staffing requirements
- Anticipated outcomes
- Dates for the deliverables

- Compensation
- Work locations
- Materials or equipment involved
- Travel involved
- Special reports

After reviewing all the work, sit down and take all things into consideration and draft up your scope of work. If you have limited staff, it will be your responsibility to write the SOW. However, it may be a good idea to acquire the expertise of a professional writer or lawyer with experience drafting a contract. They will have the ability to project the financial requirements and resources necessary for the successful execution of the project.

Also, pay close attention to details on how you will complete the work. Write down all the details and what is required to complete the project. Think about all the variables from the staffing required to the cost of materials. Give careful consideration to any risk that may be involved with the project. What are the financial or legal risk to your

company and workers? What happens if one of your workers is hurt falling off a ladder or someone steals equipment from the project? Think about any risks associated with the project and would you or the prime contractor be liable.

The following are considerations that are important for preparing a scope of work:

- Description of work
- Purpose
- Anticipated completion dates
- Project objectives
- Deliverables
- Staffing requirements
- Materials and supplies
- Key assumptions

- Pricing/Budget

**RFP Steps For A Prime Contract**

Are you ready and have the capacity to pursue a prime contract and submit a bid. If so, the following table includes a list of strategies that will get you ready for opportunities: The following is a only a checklist, as you prepare the document, you may need additional steps to insure a smooth process for the submission.

**STEP #1: RFP PROPOSAL PREPARATION**

|   |   |
|---|---|
|   | Review and download a copy of the bid package |
|   | Thoroughly review with your business team |
|   | Review the contents of the package |
|   | Determine what information is required to complete the bid package |
|   | Evaluate to determine if you have the financial and management capacity |
|   | If ready to proceed, prepare a plan of action to submit and put in place the support system |

**STEP #2: CAPACITY – SUPPORT TEAM**

|   |   |
|---|---|
|   | Will you pursue a teaming partner |
|   | Identify potential teaming/joint venture partner(s) |
|   | Prepare teaming agreements, negotiate and confirm partners |
|   | Do you need a subcontracting plan |
|   | Define staff support/team member participation |
|   | Will you need consultants/additional staff |
|   | Hold strategy meeting to further define goals |
|   | Develop a clear strategy for pursuing opportunity with team |

## STEP #3: PROPOSAL PREPARATION

|   | |
|---|---|
|   | Prepare an outline |
|   | Break down the technical sections and identify writers/team members to work on a section |
|   | Prepare a check list for all the required proposal documents |
|   | Research the government agency requesting the bid and study the acronyms appropriate for the agency |
|   | Develop a schedule with timelines for the completion of each section |
|   | Identify appropriate team member/consultant to complete specific section |
|   | Develop a system for editing and reviewing the document during the process |
|   | Set up system to communicate via email with proposals team |
|   | Insure that technology/software is in place |

## STEP #4: STAFF SUPPORT & CONSULTANTS

|   | |
|---|---|
|   | Determine staffing requirements and long term personnel |
|   | Develop a system to track candidates |
|   | Prepare offer letters, recruit staff and consultants |
|   | Contact candidates, consultants and team required to work on proposal |
|   | Prepare a matrix to track and analyze staffing requirements and needs |

## STEP #5: FINAL STEPS

|   | |
|---|---|
|   | Rreview all the proposal sections (Narrative, pricing & technical) |
|   | Prepare table of contents |

|   | Prepare transmittal letter |
|---|---|
|   | Prepare inside cover sheet |
|   | Prepare sections |
|   | Compile and gather appendix materials |
|   | Check each page of the proposal |
|   | Compare the pages to the transmittal sheets |

**Pricing And Contracts**

A very important consideration for businesses is related to pricing. If you are conducting training, you what to price your sessions by the day or hour, etc. If you are new to contracting, you should understand the basics before you attempt to respond to a request for proposal (RFP). First, you should know the difference between direct and indirect cost. In government contracting, The FAR Part #31.205: Contract Cost Principles and Procedures, specifically outlines and distinguishing between direct and indirect costs.

When you incur an expense on a contract, it can be classified as a direct or indirect expense. Here is an explanation of the differences:

**Direct expense**: labor performed directly on the contract, travel to meeting regarding status on the project, material utilized entirely for the project, subcontractors/consultants hired to work on a project, etc.

**Indirect expense**: All indirect cost can be classified as either overhead or general and administrative (G&A). Overhead includes all indirect cost incurred for the production of goods or services.

**Contract Considerations**

As you pursue contract/business opportunities, the following is a list of considerations that are valuable for the federal marketplace and the same principles can be applied to seeking contracts within the private sector:

> **Price Set Aside Contracts the Same as Full and Open Competitions**
> If you are a small business and receive a sole source set aside contract under an 8(a) or a Hub Zone award, or if you are participating in limited competition under a small business set aside designation from the federal government, be careful not to inflate your prices because you have no competition. Remember, it is your goal to develop a long-term business relationship.

> **Types of Contracts**
> You should understand the types of contracts and the criteria for each contract type. If you are pursuing federal contracts, familiarize yourself with the **FAR Part #16** regarding the types of contracts. This chapter outlines the following contract types: fixed price, cost reimbursements, incentive, indefinite delivery, time/materials and agreements. You should carefully evaluate the risks associated with each contract type. For example, Cost Plus (CP) contracting has the lowest risk because your company will receive every dollar of the cost incurred under this type of contract.

> **Research Your Competitors**
> We encourage you to do your research and gather knowledge about your competition. Visit the GSA elibrary and review detailed information regarding the labor cost of your competitors, pricing information and overall contract information. Utilize resources to help you develop a long-term pricing strategy for your company.

> **Understand "Best Value" Source Selection**
> Government contracting officers may not always select the lowest bid as the winner. If you are submitting a bid, you should not always submit your bid based on a lower price. Government Contracting

Officers consider other factors on a weighted system. For example, if the proposal contains a unique technical approach or if the bidder demonstrates a strong past performance. The contracting officer is interested in selecting companies that are equipped to successfully perform the work associated with the contract. Refer to **FAR 14.3** and review the section titled: "Responsiveness of Bids".

> **Beware of Unallowable Costs**
> Your pricing strategy should consider the costs that are unallowable with federal contracting. There are certain costs that are deemed unallowable in federal contracting. Understand what costs are allowable and should be not be included in your cost proposal. Review **FAR#31.201**

If you are pursuing federal contracts, familiarize yourself with the Defense Contract Audit Agency (DCAA). DCAA is the agency that reviews the accounting practices for businesses receiving government contractors, including prime contractors and subcontractors. The agency reviews the accounting systems to ensure that companies comply with federal contracting rules. When the DCAA performs an audit or a pre-award survey of a government contractor, they are assessing the contractor's compliance with the Federal Acquisition Regulations (FAR).

A valuable site to view technical proposals and pricing is the GSAelibrary at the following site: www.gsaelibrary.gsa.gov.

## Site Screenshot:

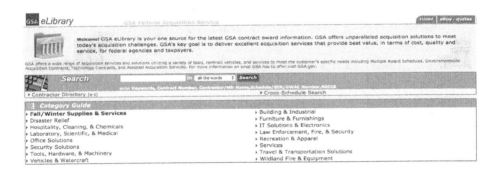

Utilize this site to research information on companies doing business with the federal government. In the search box, you can search by keywords and NAICS CODES.

Remember, you are in business to earn a profit and not lose money. The sustainability of your businesses depends on your profit margin. You need to understand your profit margin and secure financial help to keep accurate records regarding the flow of your money.

# Chapter #9: Summary

- To pursue contracts, it is critical to do the necessary preparation which includes the following: setting up a business legally, SAM registration, obtaining certifications, building performance and creating a capability statement or marketing materials.

- Invest time and preparation to get contract ready to do business with the federal government, private sector or other entities.

- If you are pursuing federal contracts, familiarize yourself with the Defense Contract Audit Agency (DCAA). DCAA is the agency that reviews the accounting practices for businesses receiving government contractors, including prime contractors and subcontractors.

- A scope of work is a formal written document that outlines specifically the work activities, deliverables and timelines involved with a project.

- Understand the difference between direct and indirect cost. In government contracting, The FAR Part #31.205: Contract Cost Principles and Procedures, specifically outlines and distinguishing between direct and indirect costs.

- Forming partnerships and joint ventures is another strategy for securing large prime contract opportunities.

# CHAPTER #10: ACTION STEPS

> What can you do to take action steps to pursue contract opportunities? We will discuss how to create a CPA, the importance of creating a plan to pursue contract opportunities. We will also discuss the concept for prospecting, creating a script and other action items.

**Contracting Plan of Action (CPA)**

A contracting plan of action (CPA) is similar to a business plan. A business plan requires you to take time to develop a detailed plan of action related to your business.

Developing your CPA encourages you to devote time to developing a strategy that specifically outlines your plan for pursuing contracts with the federal government or in the private sector.

Your response to the following questions will guide you through the process of developing a CPA for your business.

1) How much would you like to raise from securing contracts over a period of twelve months? (Set an annual goal that is realistic)

2) What is your targeted time frame for achieving your annual revenue goal? (set dates as your milestones)?

3) How will you track and monitor your goals?

4) What entities will you pursue for contract opportunities: (i.e. Federal agencies, Counties, Cities, Anchor institutions, etc.)?

5) What certifications are required for your contract prospects? (i.e. WOSB, EDWOSB, 8(a), etc)?

6) What certifications do you need to obtain and what is timeframe for completing the certification processes?

7) Do you need additional staff to support your efforts to submit bids or pursue contract opportunities?

## Communication: Scripts

When you make your approach, it is important to prepare a script that is customized to the contact. For example, If you are cold calling, include more detailed information about your company when you reach out via telephone. Provide a brief description of how you would describe your business to a potential customer. The following is a list of items that should be included in your script:

- Introduction
- Explain your business
- Depending upon who you are speaking to, curtail your script to the audience. (if you are reviewing a bid, or a forecast report, etc.)

Track all of your telephone calls, record who you speak with, and create a system to follow-up. Utilized your cold calls as a way to build a relationships.

**TIPS**: Depending upon the prospect, sometimes you will get a warm response. Don't get discouraged when you do not get a favorable response and keep working on building relationships with contracting officers and supplier diversity professionals.

## Prospecting

"Prospecting" is the term that we use for entrepreneurs researching for potential contract and business opportunities. When you are prospecting for opportunities, you should incorporate several strategies which includes conducting online research, cold calling, referrals, etc. the prospecting process requires the following tasks:

- Research for leads through the following online databases: Federal

- government Forecasting reports, Federal Procurement Database, Fed Biz Opps, press releases and business journals

- Compiling a comprehensive list of federal agencies, counties, states, business entities that you would like to pursue for potential opportunities.

- Create a system to capture and track your prospects and leads, preferably a on spread sheet.

- Monitor and track your progress on a weekly or daily basis.

- Utilize the spreadsheet as your main point of reference to evaluate your progress and follow-up.

- Keep the spreadsheets updated with your leads and other information that you obtain when you prospect. Here is an example of the headings for your spread sheet columns: outreach date, description of opportunity, contract information and follow-up.

- Share your spreadsheet with your staff and others on your team as part of the work strategy.

- Set an annual budget goal of how much you intend to raise for the entire year.

As you prospect for opportunities, remember to explore the potential to pursue opportunities in the public and private sectors. In this book, we provided you with a thorough review of how to navigate the federal contracting process. If you can master the federal contracting process, it serves as a learning process. You should always think about how you can diversify your sources of contracts. It is not a good idea to depend on one source for your revenue.

**Contract Diversification**

As you prospect for contracts, it is important that you ready for the opportunities. Let's take a moment and review the preparation required for doing business with other entities. The following table provides you with an quick overview of the strategies involved with doing business with different entities:

| Entity | Strategies |
| --- | --- |
| Doing Business with the Federal Government | <ul><li>Register your business in the System for Award Management (SAM)</li><li>Include on your website a way to showcase your information to the federal government by posting your NAICS codes and Capability statement</li><li>Review information regarding bids, and contracts posted on Federal Biz opps</li><li>Research upcoming potential contracting opportunities posted by agency on acquisition.gov</li><li>Target agencies and reach out to the Office of Small Business Disadvantaged Business Utilization (OSDBU) contracting officers.</li></ul> |
| Doing business with your local counties | <ul><li>Review requirements of your respective county regarding business licenses</li><li>Visit the county website and register your business online to do business as a vendor/supplier</li></ul> |
| Doing business with your respective State | <ul><li>Visit the website for your state and review all the requirements for doing business with the State</li><li>Follow all the required registration processes</li></ul> |

| | |
|---|---|
| Doing business with local municipalities | • Review the requirements for doing business as a vendor/supplier<br>• Visit the website and review the requirements for doing business as a vendor/supplier<br>• Complete all the processes required for doing business<br>• Review the policies or any special programs related to women in business |
| Anchor institutions | • Pursue business opportunities with local hospitals, schools, universities and colleges located in your community. |

Your prospecting strategy is to conduct research, explore databases, follow-up on leads to identify potential contract and business opportunities for your company. The overall goal is to identify potential contracts with the federal government, cities, states, municipalities, educational institutions, corporations and business entities. With any business enterprise, it is your goal to generate revenue and have enough income to sustain your business. Contracts with the federal government and in the private sector can take your business to the next level. As a process for creating your "CPA" you need to review a list of all the potential entities that are viable opportunities for securing contract opportunities.

**Marketing Tool: Capability Statements**

Think of a capability statement as your resume for your business. This document outlines important information regarding your business. If you would like to schedule a meeting with a supplier diversity professional or procurement officer, you will need to submit a Capability Statement. This is an important document and you should spend time to carefully development a statement that serves as a great representation of your business and one that details what differentiates you from your competition.

*Strategy: Think about what differentiates you from your competition and make sure you create a strong statement that represents your business. Review the capability statement from a few of your competitors.*

Take time to develop a strong capability statement that will represent your company to prospective contractors and buyers. Your capability should look professional and demonstrate that you are ready and prepared to do business. Consider having a graphic designer create your document and getting it printed on professional paper. Remember, a capability statement is a standard for federal contractors, however, corporations and private companies may not request your capability statement.

For example, if you are pursuing business in the corporate sector, the first step is to register as a vendor in the system. If you are invited to meet with Supplier Diversity professionals, you will need to prepare a professional presentation to market your company.

# CAPABILITY STATEMENT

The Capability Statement should include the following information:

1. Name of Company & Website (if applicable)

2. Point of Contact and Phone Number

3. Small Business Category (Women Owned, Service-Disabled Veteran-Owned, 8(a), Small Disadvantaged Business, etc.)

4. Statement of service and/or product being marketed to the organization

5. Product or Service Code(s)

6. NAICS Codes

7. GSA Schedule

8. DUNS Number

9. Certifications

10. DOD/Federal/State or local contracts with POC Information

11. Performance History

**WHAT YOU WILL NEED WITH YOUR CAPABILITY STATEMENT**

If you would like to schedule a meeting with a procurement officer or agency you will need to submit a Capability Statement. Think of the Capability Statement as a document similar to your resume, it will be utilized to describe your company and the services you offer.

## STRATEGY

*Think about what differentiates you from your competition and make sure you create a strong document that represents your business. Review the capability statement from one of your competitors. In addition, please provide any description that differentiates your product or service from your competitors.*

**Chapter #10: Summary**

- Work on Your Contracting Plan of Action (CPA)

- Reach out and contact procurement officers and attend networking events to build relationships with agencies

- Familiarize yourself with the terminology associated with federal contracting and the distinct differences with federal vs private contracting terminology.

- Do your research! Utilize federal databases to acquire information related to contracts awarded and potential subcontracting opportunities.

- Create several versions of your capability statement highlighting your capabilities that match the contracting opportunity.

- Do not overlook small contract opportunities which include Simplified Acquisitions as a means to get your foot in the door and build relationships with a government agency.

- Network extensively for leads (business groups, local community organizations, industry organizations

- Track your progress and marketing efforts with detailed reports that includes timeframes.

# CHAPTER #11:
# HUMAN SIDE OF BUSINESS

> An important aspect of business is the human connection that is the result of networking and building relationships. As you pursue potential contract opportunities, you are engaged in a continual process of building trust with contracting officers, prime contractors and others you are seeking to do business with. You should always communicate your value proposition to federal agencies, companies, prime contractors and potential business partners. Through your business actions, you need to demonstrate that you are in charge and capable of getting the job done!

The everyday business world is built around the "hustle and bustle" of trying to make things happen. We are constantly thinking about how we can build our customer base, who we can connect with and when will we secure our next contract. Building relationships and connections is important aspect of any business. An important business strategy is engaging in activities where you can meet face to face with potential clients, customers, partners or anyone that we would like to be a part of our business circle.

The human side of business involves the process of building valuable and trusted relationships. An important business activity is to engage in a series of "networking" strategies.

## Networking

You have probably heard the following phrase a dozen times "people do business with people they trust". As an entrepreneur, one of the most valuable skills that you can acquire is your ability to connect with others through networking. Networking is a business strategy that opens the door for potential connections and opportunities. The following outlines the important value of networking:

- Expand your list of potential clients and customers
- Connect with potential business partners
- Learn about potential contracts and business projects
- Identify potential employees or subcontractors
- Meet new friends to discuss business strategies

In the business world, valuable connections are important and can help you grow your business with opportunities. Networking is more than just handing out a business card. You don't want to be in a room randomly handing out business cards and not making a real connection that could be beneficial for your business. Here are some important business strategies that can be useful during your networking events:

- **Business Cards**
  Engage in meaningful conversations and look for commonalities that you can discuss. Do your kids attend the same school, do you enjoy playing golf, share music interests, etc.? After the exchange, if it makes sense, then exchange business cards to further the conversation or stay in touch. With this approach, you can focus on real networking and make connections that matter.

- **Image**
  Doing business events, make sure you dress in appropriate business attire. If you are not sure how to dress, you may want to Google the terms "business attire" or "business casual". Take a look of the images and make a decision about how you will dress for the event. Although, we should not be judged by the way we are dressed, people will make assumptions based upon our appearance, which is sometimes unfortunate, but we live in the real world.

- **Small Talk**
  Before you engage in a strictly business conversation, you can start with small talk. For example, this is a great event, is this your first time or I enjoyed the speaker, did you? Pull people in with small talk before you go in for the ask. Take baby steps, you want to relax them into a conversation and make yourself likeable.

- **Listen**
  The most valuable business skills that you can develop are your listening skills. Remember, people like to talk about themselves and you want to learn about who they are. Let them talk and listen to what they are saying, it can provide you with some valuable insights into who they are and how they do business.

- **Sincerity**
  Be sincerely interested in meeting people and display your interest in how you interact with them. People have a second nature and can sniff out people that are "phony and flaky".

## Networking Strategy

Develop a serious networking plan and be intentional about what you do and where you go. The overall goal is not to

waste your valuable time and you want to make real connections. Develop a networking plan based upon the following considerations:

- The Why: what are my networking goals (i.e. new clients, business or relationships)?

- The Where: where should I go (i.e. associations, events, organizations.)?

- The Cost: Budget (i.e. how much am I willing to spend and what are the returns)?

- The Benefits: Return (Who can I potential connect to and how will it benefit my business)?

- Impact: Measuring Return (How will I track and monitor my progress)?

Now it is time to do your research. You can begin with discussions with your colleagues about organizations that have been useful and impactful. As I stated, you want to be strategic and avoid wasting your time and money. Let's begin with how you think about networking. Operate on the "give and take" mentality and strategies for building relationships. Understand that you may connect with a contact and it may not result in an immediate contract. You may have to cultivate the relationship and build trust over a period. Also think about how you can be valuable to your contact. Is it a situation for you to barter services, share information or connect you to a potential resource? Position yourself to have a mutually beneficial relationship and not always receiving.

**Building Trust**

When you meet new connections and people, you must show that you are a person of character. Building a solid reputation is important and the business world is very small. If you want people to say good things about you, show integrity with all your business relationships. Here is a short list:

- Be a person of your word, if you say you are going to do something – do it!

- Treat people with respect and kindness

- Return phone calls and emails promptly

- Keep the line of communication open – even if you disagree with something

- Avoid gossip and spreading unkind words about someone

- Learn to build collaborative relationships

- Respect time – and arrive promptly for business meetings

- Acknowledge people with a thank you

## Expand Your Reach With Social Media

Utilize technology and social media to expand your social networks. Networking online can be easy through the following vehicles:

**LinkedIn**: This is a great channel to connect with other professionals. It provides a range of features that include displaying your work history, professional connections and personal recommendations.

**Google + is** powered by Google and your posts can be viewed by a wide audience.

**Twitter** – through twitter you can send short messages regarding your fields.

**Facebook** is another channel that allows you to share messages, links, videos with family, friends and contacts. This could also be a destination for people to find you.

**Blogs** are a great way for you to showcase your skills and knowledge. You can talk about a topic, share advice and provide some great information through you blog. It will require some work, to keep the blog update with information. However, you can consider posting articles written by others, as long as you list them as authors. Additionally, you can invite potential writers for you blog to help you do the work.

What is great about social media channels is that you can meet someone in another city and automatically connect with them through a social media channel. It makes reaching out and staying in touch easy! You can just log on and join someone's social network and in return, they can join yours. You can also build your network with social media online without any marketing cost!

**Your Circle**

An important business move is to always evaluate the people that are in your inner business circle. The people that you surround yourself with are very important. Who do you plan to conduct business with, get business from, or who can be valuable within your network. We constantly run into people who "talk a good game" but the reality of the situation is that they will probably never deliver. As you know, with any business, you are going to have to make decisions about what you do with your time and who you are spending your time with. The first lesson is how to avoid, what I refer to as the "flaky" People. You are out in the world networking and trying to make things happen.

It is also important to pay close attention to your intuition, the inner voice that gives you the feeling that something is not right with a situation. In business, we must to rely on our survival instincts to avoid difficult situations. When you are around people that you are unsure about, here are some signs that you should take into consideration:

- Never on time for meetings and always late
- Cancels meetings at the last minute without any notice
- You can never depend on anything that they say that they are going to do
- They seem to always be unprepared for meetings or not providing documents that you request
- Perhaps a little friendly with your clients and you seem unsure about what conversations they may have when you are not in the room

- There have been instances when you have noticed a situation that is questionable

The above list provides just a few scenarios that may cause you to have second thoughts about someone that is in your business circle. The lesson is to stay tuned into situations that do not seem right and act immediately to avoid any long term difficult business situation.

**Your Value Proposition**

Knowing your value proposition is a critical steps to understanding the potential need and profit of your business or idea. You may know have an extensive budget to pay a company to conduct extensive market research, but, here are a few simple steps that you can do yourself to engage you in a process to understand your value proposition.

- ✓ What makes you valuable as a business owner or entrepreneur?
- ✓ What qualities make you unique and attract people that want to do business with you?
- ✓ Why would people want to purchase your products or utilize your service?
- ✓ How can you build a loyal base of customers?

As we continue to emphasize throughout the book, research and planning is your best tool for preparing for contract and business opportunities. In summary, we hope that you will find the information presented in his book useful and helpful. We have included the following sections:

- ✓ Frequently Asked Questions

- ✓ Acronyms
- ✓ Glossary of Terms
- ✓ Unsolicited Proposal Format
- ✓ Business Resource Guide listing federal agencies, microloan programs and online business websites

# Real Talk: Frequently Asked Questions

I have included some questions that are asked frequently from our audience of entrepreneurs. Let's have some straight talk on FAQ's that you may find useful!

*Q. What are the benefits of a supplier diversity program?*
A. Companies focus on supplier diversity initiatives as a way to engage a pool of diverse suppliers. This provides a great opportunity for small business owners to compete for contract opportunities.

*Q. What are NAICS codes and why do I need them for my business?*
A. The North American Industry Classification System (NAICS) is a code that describes your business industry. You select and determine the best applicable codes for your business. Most business will have a primary code with secondary codes for other business activities.

*Q. What are the requirements for the WOSB & EDWOSB certification program?*
To qualify for the programs your company should be 51% directly owned by a women who is engaged actively working in the business and engaged in long term decisions and operations.

*Q. What is the certification process?*
A. Basically, the certification process requires you to submit specific documents that will confirm your gender, U.S. Citizenship, ownership is controlled by a women or minority.

*Q. Why do I need certification?*
A. The certification process confirms that your business is owned by a women/minority and the process allows you to qualify for programs that

address small business concerns. For example, when you certify with the Small Business Administration (SBA) as a Women Owned Small Business (WOSB), you now qualify for contracts opportunities set aside for women owned businesses. If you certify with the Women's Business Enterprise Network (WNENC), there are corporations that acknowledge the certifications and personally work with you to connect you to opportunities as a diverse spend. Utilize it to your advantage, do your homework and decide which certifications are best for your business. Depending on your research and what company that you want to market your goods and services to will depend on your strategy for certifications.

**Q. *The certification process is confusing, where do I begin?***
**A.** Remember, if you are a new business you may want to consider beginning your certification process with the Small Business Administration (SBA) as a Women Owned Small Business (WOSB) or an Economically Disadvantaged Women Owned Small Business (EDWOSB). You can self-certify online with the SBA at the following site: **certify.sba.gov**. The SBA certifications are free!

**Q. *How does networking and associations build your business?***
**A.** Consider all the organizations that can be advantageous for your business. For example, supplier diversity councils, Chamber of Commerce, industry type organizations related to your business. Remember, people do business with people that they like, so make it a point to connect with prospective suppliers and other business owners. Building your network and relationships can lead into potential contracts and partnership opportunities for you to do business.

**Q. *Why do some corporations put an emphasis on certifications?***
**A.** Corporations and companies have built long standing relationships with certification companies. They trust the process and are happy with the

referrals. It also helps them meet their goals of working with women and minority companies. When companies are already certified, they are more attractive because they do not have to screen the companies to insure they meet the criteria.

**Q. *I am not ready to pursue a prime contract, how can I build my business capability?***
***A.*** It may be wise for you to consider pursuing a sub-contract opportunity with a prime contractor. This is a perfect way for you to build your capability, performance and experience.

**Q. *What is the role of a Supplier Diversity Officer?***
Diversity professionals play a major role in helping you get your foot in the door. The diversity manager could open doors for you to do business with a company. They are committed to your success and if you succeed, it looks good when they bring in talented diverse companies. They will also advocate on your behalf and provide you with suggestions on how to market and best position your company for prospective opportunities.

**Q. *How are third-party certifiers different from the U.S. Small Business Administration?***
As outlined in this guide, third-party certifiers are organizations that provide business owners with a certification process. The agencies provide a fee for their services and you are usually required to renew your membership annually. The following is an example of third party certifiers:

- ✓ National Minority Supplier Development Council (NMSDC)
- ✓ The Women's Business Enterprise National Council (WNENC)

Both of the entities have chapters and regional partnering organizations that cover 50 states.

**Q. Does the SBA recommend third party certifiers?**
Yes, the SBA has a list of approved third-party certifiers that meet the requirements of the WOSB program. Only SBA-approved third party certifiers (TPC's) can give you an authorized "certificate" of eligibility as a WOSB or EDWOSB. The following is a listing of the four SBA-approved TPCs.

- **El Paso Hispanic Chamber of Commerce**
- **National Women Business Owners Corporation**
- **US Women's Chamber of Commerce**
- **Women's Business Enterprise National Council (WBENC)**

Remember, you can obtain a SBA certification and it is free. There are fees associated with third party certifiers. You can go online and certify your business with the Small Business Administration. Review the SBA certifications and the criteria for each of the certifications online at certify.sba.gov.!

# APPENDICES

## Acronyms: Federal Contracting

| Term | |
|---|---|
| ADO | Administrative Center Officer |
| ADA | American Disabilities Act |
| B & P | Bid and Proposal |
| BOA | Business Office Administrator |
| BPA | Blanket Purchase Agreement |
| CA | Cooperative Agreement |
| CIO | Chief Information Officer |
| CO | Contracting Officer |
| COB | Close of Business |
| CY | Calendar Year |
| DCAA | Defense Contract Audit Agency |
| DLH | Direct Labor Hour |
| DOC | Department of Commerce |
| DOD | Department of Defense |
| DOE | Department of Energy |
| DOI | Department of Interior |
| DOJ | Department of Justice |
| DOS | Department of State |
| DUNS | Data Universal Numbering System |
| DVD | Director Vendor Development |
| EC | Electronic Commerce |
| EEOC | Equal Employment Opportunity |
| EO | Executive Order |
| ETA | Established Time of Arrival |
| FAR | Federal Acquisition Regulation |
| FLSA | Fair Labor Standard Act |
| FMV | Fair Market Value |

| | |
|---|---|
| FPL | Federal Procurement List |
| FY | Fiscal Year |
| GAA | General Agency Agreement |
| GAI | Government Accounting |
| HUB | Historically Utilized Business |
| IQC | Indefinite Quality Contract |
| LOP | Letter of Procurement |
| MBDC | Minority Business Development Center |
| MOA | Memorandum of Agreement |
| MOU | Memorandum of Understanding |
| NAICS | North American Industry Classification Codes |
| PO | Purchase Order |
| OMB | Office of Management Budget |
| OPM | Office of Personnel Management |
| OSDBU | Office of Small Disadvantaged Business Utilization |
| OSHA | Office of Safety Hazard Administration |
| OWBO | Office of Women's Business Ownership |
| PCR | Procurement Center Report |
| POC | Point of Contact |
| R & D | Research & Development |
| RFB | Request for Bid |
| RFP | Request for Proposal |
| SBA | Small Business Administration |
| SBDA | Small Business Development Agency |
| SBSA | Small Business Set Aside |
| SDB | Small Disadvantaged Business |
| SDV | Small Disadvantaged Veteran |
| SDVOSB | Small Disadvantaged Veteran Owned Small Business |
| SOW | Statement of Work |
| SF | Standard Form |

| SOP | Standard Operating Procedures |
|---|---|
| TPIN | Tax Payer Identification Number |
| VSS | Vendor Support System |
| WBC | Women's Business Center |
| WBE | Women's Business Enterprise |
| WOSB | Women's Owned Small Business |
| YTD | Year To Date |

## Glossary of Terms

**Certification:**
The process of submitting documentation to the SBA or a third-party certifier to confirm that you are a woman, minority owned or veteran owned business. Submitting the documentation will allow you to be in a socioeconomic status and eligible for special programs, set asides and sole source contract opportunities.

**Clause:** A term or condition the is included in contracts or solicitations that outlines a specific condition.

**Contingency Fee**: Agreed upon fee that is a commission or percentage based upon the awarding of success of a contract. this fee is included in the agreement.

**Contract** - In law, a contract is a binding legal agreement that is enforceable in a court of law or by binding arbitration.

**Cooperative Agreement**: A legal agreement/instrument that outlines the relationship with the government and business to perform specific activities.

**Demographics** - Demographic data are the characteristics of a human population based on factors such as age, race, sex, economic status, level of education, income level and employment, among others.

**Defence Contract Audit Agency (DCAA)**
DCAA is the agency that reviews the accounting practices for businesses receiving government contractors, including prime contractors and subcontractors. The agency reviews the accounting systems to ensure that companies comply with federal contracting rules. When the DCAA performs an audit or a pre-award survey of a government contractor, they are assessing the contractor's compliance with the Federal Acquisition Regulations (FAR).

**Disadvantaged Business Enterprise (DBE)**
A for profit small business concern that is a minimum of 51 percent owned by individuals that are economically disadvantaged.

**Disclosure** - The act of releasing all relevant information pertaining to a company that may influence an investment decision.

**Doing Business As** (DBA) is the use of a fictitious business name to trade under in business. DBA allows a person to legally do business under a different name, without having to create a completely new business entity.

**D-U-N-S Number**
A unique nine-digit identification number for your business. The assignment of the number is free and required for businesses seeking to secure federal contracts.

**E-learning** - electronic-based training, allows you to learn anywhere and usually at any time, as long as you have a properly configured computer.

**Federal Acquisition Regulation (FAR)**
A principal set of rules in the Federal Acquisition Regulation System. This system consists of sets of regulations issued by
agencies of the Federal Government to govern what is called the "acquisition process"; this is the process through which the government purchases ("acquires") goods and services.

**Freedom of Information Act** (FOIA)
The government operates in transparency and the FOIA allows for the public the right to request access to federal agency records or **information** except. The access to information can be denied it is protected from disclosure by any of nine exemptions contained in the law or by one of three special law enforcement record exclusions.

## Forecasting Reports
The federal government informs vendors of future contracting opportunities through online reports published by various government agencies. This information is made available pursuant to the Business Opportunity Development Reform Act of 1988 (Public Law 100-656).

## Goal
A business or government/education entity that has a supplier/vendor plan that establishes percentage goals for specific business categories. For example, the federal government set a goal of 5 percent of contracts should be awarded to woman-owned small businesses and small disadvantaged businesses.

## General Services Administration (GSA)
GSA delivers high quality, cost effective services in real estate, acquisition, and technology for customers across the federal government.

## GSA Schedule
GSA Schedule Contracts, also known as Federal Supply Schedules, are indefinite delivery, indefinite quantity (IDIQ), long-term contracts under the General Services Administration's Multiple Award Schedule (MAS) Program.

## HUBZone (Historically Underutilized Business Zone)
HUBZone is a United States Small Business Administration (SBA) program for small companies that operate and employ people in HUBZone areas. The program was created in response to the HUBZone empowerment Act created by the US Congress in 1998.

**Minority Business Enterprise (MBE)** – A term which is defined as a business which is at least 51% owned, operated and controlled daily by one or more (in combination) American citizens of certain ethnic minority classifications.

**Minority Owned Business (MOB)** - A for-profit enterprise, regardless of size, physically located in the United States or its trust territories, which is owned, operated and controlled by minority group members.

**Mobile Marketing** - The systematic planning, implementing and control of a mix of business activities intended to bring together buyers and sellers for the mutually advantageous exchange or transfer of products where the primary point of contact with the consumer is via their mobile device.

## NAICS Codes

North American Identification Classification System (NAICS) code is required for administrative, contracting and tax purposes. For federal contracting, business owners are required to identify in the CCR all the NAICS codes applicable to their business.

## Ostensible Subcontractor Rule

Federal regulations limit the percentage of a set-aside contract that a prime contractor may subcontract to other concerns. An ostensible contractor affiliation occurs when a small business holds a prime contract, however, a subcontractor is hired for the job and is the company that actually performs most of the work.

**Office of Small Disadvantage Business Utilization (OSDBU)** - was created as part of the Small Business Act (SBA) to ensure that small and disadvantaged businesses are provided maximum practicable opportunity to participate in the agency's contracting process.

**Outsourcing** – The process of contracting with outside vendors/suppliers to perform work for your company or a scope of work under a contract.

**Prime Contractors** – Company bids and wins a contract and responsible for performing the work and assuming the full responsibility for the completion of the contract from start to finish.

**Procurement** – A process for buying or securing goods and services from a supplier/vendor.

**Purchase Order**
A legally binding document between a supplier and a buyer that details the items and price a buyer agrees to purchase.

**Purchasing** - Management control point where all significant purchases are monitored for the right authorization of the right item, at the right price, quality, and quantity, from the right supplier at the right terms, and at the right time.

**Request for Proposal (RFP)** - Document used in sealed-bid procurement procedures through which a purchaser advises the potential suppliers of (1) statement and scope of work, (2) specifications, (3) schedules or timelines, (4) contract type, (5) data requirements, (6) terms and conditions, (7) description of goods and/or services to be procured, (8) general criteria used in evaluation procedure, (9) special contractual requirements, (10) technical goals, (11) instructions for preparation of technical, management, and/or cost proposals.

**Responsible Bidder**: A business entity that has the full capacity to perform the contract requirements. The variables considered when evaluating a responsible bidder include solid past performance, financial capability, contract experience, personnel, technical skills, infrastructure, etc.

**Scope of Work** - A scope of work sets forth requirements for performance of work to achieve contract objectives. The scope of work must be clear, accurate and complete.

**Small Business Concern (SBC)**
A business that is independently operated and owned and qualifies as a small business based on the criteria and size standards set by the U.S. government.

## Sole Source Contract
The term "**no-bid contract**" is a popular phrase for what is officially known as a "sole source contract". U.S. law permits the government to award sole source contracts under specified circumstances.

**Small Disadvantaged Business (SDB)** –Businesses as defined by the SBA meeting specific guidelines are referred to as disadvantaged.

**Small Disadvantaged Veteran Owned Small Business (SDVOSB)** – A program with established criteria that is used to provide sole source and set aside procurement opportunities for Veteran owned small businesses.

## Service Disabled Veteran Owned Small Business (SDVOSB)
A small business concern that is at least 51 percent or more owned, operated and controlled by veterans that are disabled.

**Subcontractors** - Junior or secondary contractor who contracts with a prime contractor (and not the principal or owner of the project) to perform some or all the prime contractor's contractual-obligations under the prime contract.

## Subnet
A website where prime contractors post opportunities for subcontractors.

## Supplier Diversity
A business program that encourages the use of: minority-owned, women owned, veteran owned, service disabled
veteran owned, historically underutilized business, and SBA defined small business vendors as suppliers.

## System for Award Management (SAM)
The primary database for vendors seeking to do business with the federal government. Federal Acquisitions Regulations (FAR) require all prospective

vendors to be registered in SAM prior to the award of a contract, basic agreement, basic ordering agreement, or blanket purchase agreement.

## SWOT Analysis
Situation analysis in which internal strengths and weaknesses of an organization, and external opportunities and threats faced by it are closely examined to chart a strategy.

## Value Proposition
A clear statement that articulates how your product solves problems, delivers specific benefits to customers and why you are different from your competitors.

## Vendor Diversity
To create and implement initiatives that will increase procurement opportunities for small and minorities business.

## Women Business Enterprise (WBE)
A woman owned business is at least 51 percent or more owned by a woman.

**Women Owned Business Certification** – A process that validates that the business is 51 percent owned, controlled, operated, and managed by a woman or women. To achieve
Certification, women owned businesses complete a formal documentation and site visit process which is administered by an organization such as the Women Business Council.

**Sections: Federal Bid Package**

The first step to pursuing a prime contract is to complete a Request for Proposal (RFP). The typical RFP is a document with very specific requirements. Federal government RFP formats are mandated by the Federal Acquisition Regulation (FAR).

The following is a listing of the sections in a typical federal RFP:
- Section A. Information to Offerors or Quoters
- Section B. Supplies or Services and Price/Costs
- Section C. Statement of Work (SOW)
- Section D. Packages and Marking
- Section E. Inspection and Acceptance
- Section F. Deliveries or Performance
- Section G. Contract Administrative Data
- Section H. Special Contract Requirements
- Section I. Contract Clauses/General Provisions
- Section J. Attachments, Exhibits
- Section K. Representations/Certifications and Statements of Offerors
- Section L. Proposal Preparation Instructions and Other
- Section M. Evaluation Criteria

**Federal Unsolicited Proposal Format**

**DEFINITION**

An "unsolicited proposal" means a written proposal for a new or innovative idea that is submitted to an agency on the initiative of the offeror for the purpose of obtaining a contract with the Government, and that is NOT in response to a Request for Proposals, Broad Agency Announcement, Small Business Innovation Research topic, Small Business Technology Transfer Research topic, Program Research and Development announcement, or any other Government-initiated solicitation or program.

**FAR 15.605 Content of unsolicited proposals.**

Unsolicited proposals should contain the following information to permit consideration in an objective and timely manner:

1. (a) Basic information including-
   a. (1) Offeror's name and address and type of organization; E.G.,profit, nonprofit, educational, small business;
   b. (2) Names and telephone numbers of technical and business personnel to be contacted for evaluation or negotiation purposes;
   c. (3) Identification of proprietary data to be used only for evaluation purposes;
   d. (4) Names of other Federal, State, or local agencies or parties receiving the proposal or funding the proposed effort;
   e. (5) Date of submission; and
   f. (6) Signature of a person authorized to represent and contractually obligate the offeror.
2. (b) Technical information including-
   a. (1) Concise title and abstract (approximately 200 words) of the proposed effort;
   b. (2) A reasonably complete discussion stating the objectives of the effort or activity, the method of approach and extent of effort to be employed, the nature and extent of the

anticipated results, and the manner in which the work will help to support accomplishment of the agency's mission;

c. (3) Names and biographical information on the offeror's key personnel who would be involved, including alternates; and

d. (4) Type of support needed from the agency; E.G.,Government property or personnel resources.

3. (c) Supporting information including-

a. (1) Proposed price or total estimated cost for the effort in sufficient detail for meaningful evaluation;

b. (2) Period of time for which the proposal is valid (a 6-month minimum is suggested);

c. (3) Type of contract preferred;

d. (4) Proposed duration of effort;

e. (5) Brief description of the organization, previous experience, relevant past performance, and facilities to be used;

f. (6) Other statements, if applicable, about organizational conflicts of interest, security clearances, and environmental impacts; and

g. (7) The names and telephone numbers of agency technical or other agency points of contact already contacted regarding the proposal.

## VALID UNSOLICITED PROPOSAL

A valid unsolicited proposal must:

• Be innovative and unique;

• Be independently originated and developed by the offeror. Unsolicited proposals in response to a publicized general statement of agency needs are considered to be independently originated;

• Be prepared without Government supervision, endorsement, direction, or direct Government involvement;

- Include sufficient detail to permit a determination that Government support could be worthwhile and the proposed work could benefit the agency's research and development or other mission responsibilities;

- Not be an advance proposal for a known agency requirement that can be acquired by competitive methods; and

- Not address a previously published agency requirement.

## OTHER CONSIDERATIONS

Only warranted Contracting Officers have authority to contractually bind the Government. Technical personnel who may receive, handle, or evaluate unsolicited proposals are not authorized to commit the Government.

Offerors submitting unsolicited proposals that meet the regulatory requirements & receive a favorable comprehensive evaluation may only receive award after the contracting officer:

- Makes an affirmative determination of an offeror's responsibility (FAR Subpart 9.1);

- Considers Organizational Conflicts of Interest issues (FAR Subpart 9.5);

- Ensures sufficient funds are available for award;

- Complies with synopsis requirements of FAR Subpart 5.2; and

- Executes any determination & finding or justification and obtained any approval(s) required by FAR Subpart 6.3.

In the event the proposal is not accepted, the Government is not obligated in any way to reimburse the offeror for any cost that may have been incurred in preparing & submitting the unsolicited proposal.

## PROPRIETARY INFORMATION

An unsolicited proposal may include data that the offeror does not want disclosed to the public for any purpose or used by the Government except for evaluation purposes. If the offeror wishes to restrict the data, the proposal must be marked with the following as required by FAR 15.609:

- Title Page:

"Use and Disclosure of Data This proposal includes data that shall not be disclosed outside the Government and shall not be duplicated, used or disclosed – in whole or in part – for any purpose other than to evaluate this proposal. However, if a contract is awarded to this offeror as a result of – or in connection with – the submission of these data, the Government shall have the right to duplicate, use, or disclose the data to the extent provided in the resulting contract. This restriction does not limit the Government's right to use information contained in these data if they are obtained from another source without restriction. The data subject to this restriction are contained in Sheets [insert numbers or other identification of sheets]."

• Each sheet of data the offeror wishes to restrict:

"Use or disclosure of data contained on this sheet is subject to the restriction on the title page of this proposal."

# Form: Request for Quotation

# Form: Solicitation, Offer & Award

| SOLICITATION, OFFER AND AWARD | 1. THIS CONTRACT IS A RATED ORDER UNDER DPAS (15 CFR 700) | | RATING | PAGE | OF | PAGES |
|---|---|---|---|---|---|---|
| 2. CONTRACT NUMBER | 3. SOLICITATION NUMBER | 4. TYPE OF SOLICITATION<br>☐ SEALED BID (IFB)<br>☐ NEGOTIATED (RFP) | 5. DATE ISSUED | 6. REQUISITION/PURCHASE NUMBER | | |
| 7. ISSUED BY | CODE | 8. ADDRESS OFFER TO (If other than Item 7) | | | | |

NOTE: In sealed bid solicitations "offer" and "offeror" mean "bid" and "bidder".

## SOLICITATION

9. Sealed offers in original and _____ copies for furnishing the supplies or services in the Schedule will be received at the place specified in item 8, or if hand carried, in the depository located in _____ until _____ local time _____ (Hour) (Date)

CAUTION - LATE Submissions, Modifications, and Withdrawals: See Section L, Provision No. 52.214-7 or 52.215-1. All offers are subject to all terms and conditions contained in this solicitation.

| 10. FOR INFORMATION CALL: | A. NAME | B. TELEPHONE (NO COLLECT CALLS) | | C. E-MAIL ADDRESS |
|---|---|---|---|---|
| | | AREA CODE | NUMBER EXTENSION | |

## 11. TABLE OF CONTENTS

| (X) | SEC | DESCRIPTION | PAGE(S) | (X) | SEC | DESCRIPTION | PAGE(S) |
|---|---|---|---|---|---|---|---|
| | | PART I - THE SCHEDULE | | | | PART II - CONTRACT CLAUSES | |
| | A | SOLICITATION/CONTRACT FORM | | | I | CONTRACT CLAUSES | |
| | B | SUPPLIES OR SERVICES AND PRICES/COSTS | | | | PART III - LIST OF DOCUMENTS, EXHIBITS AND OTHER ATTACH. | |
| | C | DESCRIPTION/SPECS./WORK STATEMENT | | | J | LIST OF ATTACHMENTS | |
| | D | PACKAGING AND MARKING | | | | PART IV - REPRESENTATIONS AND INSTRUCTIONS | |
| | E | INSPECTION AND ACCEPTANCE | | | K | REPRESENTATIONS, CERTIFICATIONS AND OTHER STATEMENTS OF OFFERORS | |
| | F | DELIVERIES OR PERFORMANCE | | | | | |
| | G | CONTRACT ADMINISTRATION DATA | | | L | INSTRUCTIONS, CONDITIONS, AND NOTICES TO OFFERORS | |
| | H | SPECIAL CONTRACT REQUIREMENTS | | | M | EVALUATION FACTORS FOR AWARD | |

### OFFER (Must be fully completed by offeror)

NOTE: Item 12 does not apply if the solicitation includes the provisions at 52.214-16, Minimum Bid Acceptance Period.

12. In compliance with the above, the undersigned agrees, if this offer is accepted within _____ calendar days (60 calendar days unless a different period is inserted by the offeror) from the date for receipt of offers specified above, to furnish any or all items upon which prices are offered at the set opposite each item, delivered at the designated point(s), within the time specified in the schedule.

| 13. DISCOUNT FOR PROMPT PAYMENT<br>(See Section I, Clause No. 52.232-8) | 10 CALENDAR DAYS (%) | 20 CALENDAR DAYS (%) | 30 CALENDAR DAYS (%) | CALENDAR DAYS(%) |
|---|---|---|---|---|
| 14. ACKNOWLEDGMENT OF AMENDMENTS<br>(The offeror acknowledges receipt of amendments to the SOLICITATION for offerors and related documents numbered and dated): | AMENDMENT NO. | DATE | AMENDMENT NO. | DATE |

| 15A. NAME AND ADDRESS OF OFFER- OR | | CODE | | FACILITY | | 16. NAME AND THE TITLE OF PERSON AUTHORIZED TO SIGN OFFER<br>(Type or print) |
|---|---|---|---|---|---|---|
| 15B. TELEPHONE NUMBER<br>AREA CODE NUMBER EXTENSION | | | 15C. CHECK IF REMITTANCE ADDRESS IS DIFFERENT FROM ABOVE - ENTER SUCH ADDRESS IN SCHEDULE | | 17. SIGNATURE | 18. OFFER DATE |

### AWARD (To be completed by Government)

| 19. ACCEPTED AS TO ITEMS NUMBERED | 20. AMOUNT | 21. ACCOUNTING AND APPROPRIATION | | |
|---|---|---|---|---|
| 22. AUTHORITY FOR USING OTHER THAN FULL OPEN COMPETITION:<br>☐ 10 U.S.C. 2304 (c) ( ) ☐ 41 U.S.C. 3304(a) ( ) | | 23. SUBMIT INVOICES TO ADDRESS SHOWN IN<br>(4 copies unless otherwise specified) | | ITEM |
| 24. ADMINISTERED BY (If other than Item 7) | | 25. PAYMENT WILL BE MADE BY | | CODE |
| 26. NAME OF CONTRACTING OFFICER (Type or print) | | 27. UNITED STATES OF AMERICA<br>(Signature of Contracting Officer) | | 28. AWARD DATE |

IMPORTANT - Award will be made on this Form, or on Standard Form 26, or by other authorized official written notice.

AUTHORIZED FOR LOCAL REPRODUCTION
Previous edition is unusable

**STANDARD FORM 33** (REV. 6/2014)
Prescribed by GSA - FAR (48 CFR) 53.214 (c)

# BUSINESS RESOURCE GUIDE

## Small Business Administration

The Small Business Administration (SBA) was on July 30, 1953. The SBA has been instrumental in providing entrepreneurs and small business community with millions of loans, loan guarantees, contracts, counseling sessions and other forms of technical assistance. The SBA delivers programs in the following areas:

- Education and entrepreneurial development assistance and training
- Access to capital with business and micro-lending
- Processing of certifications for women and small businesses
- Educational workshops on SBA certifications
- Specialized training and SCORE coaching

The following is a listing of the offices by region.

- Region I
- SBA New England - Serving Connecticut, Maine, Massachusetts, New Hampshire, Rhode Island and Vermont
- Region II
- SBA Atlantic - Serving New York, New Jersey, Puerto Rico, and The U.S. Virgin Islands
- Region III
- SBA Mid-Atlantic - Serving Delaware, Maryland, Pennsylvania, Virginia, Washington, DC, and West Virginia
- Region IV
- SBA Southeast - Serving Alabama, Florida, Georgia, Kentucky, Mississippi, North Carolina, South Carolina, and Tennessee
- Region V
- SBA Great Lakes - Serving Illinois, Indiana, Michigan, Minnesota, Ohio, and Wisconsin
- Region VI
- SBA South Central - Serving Arkansas, Louisiana, New Mexico, Oklahoma, and Texas
- Region VII
- SBA Great Plains - Serving Iowa, Kansas, Missouri, and Nebraska
- Region VIII
- SBA Rocky Mountains - Serving Colorado, Montana, North Dakota, South Dakota, Utah, and Wyoming
- Region IX
- SBA Pacific - Serving Arizona, California, Guam, Hawaii, and Nevada
- Region X
- SBA Pacific Northwest - Serving Alaska, Idaho, Oregon, and Washington

*The SBA also a listing of district offices located in various states. You can visit the SBA site to get the location of your local Georgia District Office. Here is a sample of the site:*

*Visit the SBA site to get the address and contact information for your local office.*

*If you live in Georgia, here is information for the Georgia District Office*
233 Peachtree Street, NE
Suite #300
Atlanta, GA 30303
United States
Phone: 404-331-0100


### Small Business Development Centers (SBDC)

Small Business Development Centers (SBDCs) provide a range of technical assistance to small businesses and aspiring entrepreneurs. The program remains one of the nation's largest small business assistance programs in the federal government. The SBDCs are made up of a unique collaboration of SBA federal funds, state and local governments, and private sector resources.
SBDCs provide participants with the following services: development

of business plans; manufacturing assistance; financial packaging and lending assistance; exporting and importing support; disaster recovery assistance; procurement and contracting aid; market research services; aid to 8(a) firms in all stages; and healthcare information.
SBDC assistance is available virtually anywhere with 63 Host networks branching out with more than 900 service delivery points throughout the U.S., the District of Columbia, Guam, Puerto Rico, American Samoa and the U.S. Virgin Islands,. The 63 SBDC hosts include:

- 48 University-sponsored SBDC Hosts: 2 2 University Hosts are in Washington, DC (Howard University) , and the U.S. Virgin Islands (the University of the Virgin Islands)8 Community college-sponsored SBDC hosts: Dallas-TX, UT, OR, NM, AZ, San Diego-CA, Los Angeles-CA, and American Samoa

- 8 Community college-sponsored SBDC hosts: Dallas-TX, UT, OR, NM, AZ, San Diego-CA, Los Angeles-CA, and American Samoa

- 7 State-sponsored Lead SBDCs (CO, IL, IN, MN, MT, OH, & WV): SINCE 1990, CONGRESS HAS REQUIRED ALL NEW SBDCS BE HOSTED BY INSTITUTIONS OF HIGHER EDUCATION OR WOMEN'S BUSINESS CENTERS

*SOURCE: WWW.SBA.GOV*

**Office of Small and Disadvantaged Business Utilization (OSDBU)**

Many federal agencies have a dedicated office to help small businesses search and compete for contract opportunities within the agency. These offices are known as either an Office of Small and Disadvantaged Business Utilization (OSDBU) or an Office of Small Business

Programs (OSBP). They may hold informational trainings and outreach events, or provide contact information for businesses to use to ask questions about contracting with their agencies.
Defense Contract Management Agency
Small Business Programs
http://www.dcma.mil/smallbusiness/

**Department of Defense**
Office of Small Business Programs
http://business.defense.gov

**Defense Information Systems Agency**
Office of Small Business Programs
http://www.disa.mil

U.S. Department of Defense Education Activity/ Small Business Programs
http://www.dodea.edu/offices/procurement/index.cfm

Department of Commerce
Office of Small and Disadvantaged Business Utilization (OSDBU)
usec.doc.gov

Federal Deposit Insurance Corporation
Division of Administration
https://www.fdic.gov/buying/goods/

General Services Administration
Office of Small Business Utilization
https://www.gsa.gov/smallbusiness

Minority Business Development Agency
Office of Small Business Development
https://www.mbda.gov

National Aeronautics and Space Administration
Office of Small Business Programs
http://www.osbp.nasa.gov

National Science Foundation
Office of Small and Disadvantaged Business Utilization
https://www.nsf.gov/about/contracting/osdbu.jsp

Smithsonian Institution
Supplier Diversity Program
https://www.si.edu/oeema/supplierdiversity

Social Security Administration
Office of Small and Disadvantaged Business Utilization
https://www.ssa.gov/agency/osdbu

U.S. Agency for International Development
Office of Small and Disadvantaged Business Utilization
https://www.usaid.gov/business/small_business/

U.S. Department of Agriculture
Office of Small and Disadvantaged Business Utilization
https://www.dm.usda.gov/smallbus/index.php

U.S. Department of Commerce
Office of Small and Disadvantaged Business Utilization
http://www.osec.doc.gov/osdbu/

U.S. Department of Energy
Office of Small and Disadvantaged Business Utilization

www.smallbusiness.energy.gov

U.S. Department of Health and Human Services
Office of Small and Disadvantaged Business Utilization
http://www.hhs.gov

U.S. Department of Homeland Security
Office of Small and Disadvantaged Business Utilization
https://www.dhs.gov/do-business-dhs

U.S. Department of Housing and Urban Development
Office of Small and Disadvantaged Business Utilization
http://www.hud.gov/smallbusiness

U.S. Department of Interior
Office of Small and Disadvantaged Business Utilization
https://www.doi.gov/pmb/osdbu

U.S. Department of Justice
Office of Small and Disadvantaged Business Utilization
https://www.justice.gov/osdbu

U.S. Department of Labor
Office of Small and Disadvantaged Business Utilization
https://www.dol.gov/oasam/programs/osdbu/regs/procurement.htm

Department of State
Office of Small and Disadvantaged Business Utilization
https://www.state.gov/s/dmr/sdbu/

U.S. Department of Transportation
Office of Small and Disadvantaged Business Utilization
https://www.transporation.gov/osdbu/

U.S. Department of the Treasury
Office of Small and Disadvantaged Business Utilization
https://www.treasury.gov/osdbu

U.S. Department of Veterans Affairs
Office of Small and Disadvantaged Business Utilization
http://www.va.gov/osdbu

U.S. Office of Personnel Management
Office of Small and Disadvantaged Business Utilization
https://www.opm.gov

U.S. Postal Service
Supplier Diversity Supply Management Strategies
http://about.usps.com

**Score-Core of Retired Executives**

SCORE is a national network of nearly 14,000 entrepreneurs, business leaders and executives who volunteer as mentors to America's small businesses. SCORE has helped more than 8.5 million entrepreneurs nationwide by leveraging decades of expertise from seasoned business professionals to help entrepreneurs start businesses, grow companies and create jobs in local communities.

For additional information regarding SCORE, visit the following website: www.score.org

If you live in Georgia, here is the address:

*Atlanta SCORE* **#0048**
1720 Peachtree Road, NW
6th Floor
Atlanta, GA 30309
Phone:(404) 347-2442
Fax: (404) 347-1227

**Minority Business Development Agency (MBDA)**

The MBDA is a great resource for minority and women owned businesses seeking to enter new markets and expand. The business experts can assist with a range of business topics and provide information on securing capital, contracts and how to do business globally. MBDA Centers are located in areas with the largest concentration of minority populations and the largest number of minority businesses.

To identify a MBDA, visit the following site and utilize locator at https://mbda.gov. You can input your city, state and zip code and it will locate a MBDA agency in your city.

*MBDA Regional Office*
401 W. Peachtree Street, NW, Suite 1715
Atlanta, GA 30308
Phone: (404) 730-3300
Fax: (404) 730-3313

**Microloans Programs**

The *Microloan* program provides small loans ranging from under $500 to $50,000 to women, low-income, minority, veteran, and other small business owners through a network of approximately 160 intermediaries nationwide. Under this program, the SBS makes funds available to nonprofit intermediaries that, in turn, make the small loans directly to entrepreneurs, including veterans. Proceeds can be used for typical business purposes such as working capital, or the purchase of furniture, fixtures, machinery, supplies equipment, and inventory.

Microloans may not be used for the purchase of real estate. Interest rates are negotiated between the borrower and the intermediary. The maximum term for a microloan is 7 years. The SBA has micro-lending programs, however, if you don't have a local SBA intermediary in your area, the following is a list of alternative micro lending providers:

- **Access to Capital for Entrepreneurs (ACE)**
  **www.aceloans.org**

ACE is an SBA Microloan Intermediary, a USDA Intermediary Relender and a certified Community Development Financial Institution (CDFI). Operation as a CDFI means creating jobs and opportunities for low income and under-served populations while executing sound financial and portfolio management.

- **Accion USA  us.accion.org**

Accion is a global non-profit organization based in Brooklyn, New York, with a mission to give people worldwide the financial tools they need to grow healthy businesses.

- **PayPal Working Capital**
  **www.paypal.com/workingcapital**

Online sellers and customers alike recognize PayPal as the world's leading online payment processing service. In 2013, PayPal launched PayPal Working Capital, offering microloans to a select number of PayPal sellers.

- **Kiva     www.kiva.org**

Kiva works both globally and domestically, providing interest-free microloans for up to $100,000. In order to qualify, you must first have a family or friend lend to your venture.

- **LiftFund   www.liftfund.com**

LiftFund offers microloans in the southern part of the United States—think Texas, Louisiana, Mississippi, Alabama, Arkansas, Missouri, Kentucky, and
Tennessee.

- **Grameen America  www.grameenamerica.org**

Grameen America is an international organization that makes microloans to businesses operating in poor communities. Grameen America is especially known for helping women business owners succeed in disadvantaged areas.

## Online Business Resources

| | |
|---|---|
| Women Owned Small Business Certification<br>certify.sba.gov | A new modernized site for self-certification as a Women Owned Small Business (WOSB). The portal provides a login and self-registration process. |
| System for Award Management<br>www.sam.gov | In order to be considered for contract opportunities your business is required to complete this online registration process. |
| SBA Size Standard Tool<br>sba.gov/tools/size-standards | An online assessment tool to determine if your business fits within the guidelines of being categorized as a small business concern. |
| U.S. Small Business Administration<br>www.sba.gov | A one stop extensive portal providing business resources on the topics of business plans, contracting, small business concerns, and laws and regulations. This site also links to other government sites and resources for small businesses. |
| U.S. Small Business Administration Learning Center | An online training portal on extensive business topics. |

sba.gov/tools/sba-learning-center

Business.gov
www.business.gov

A website that connects business to resources and information applicable to small businesses. This site provides great educational online tools on a variety of business topics to include contracting, taxes, financing, etc. The site also features an online training portal with over 200 online courses, videos, webinars and transcripts.

Women Owned Small Business Centers
www.sba.gov

The SBA has a network of Women's Business Centers throughout the United States. The WBC's are designed to provide women with training and education to help develop and expand business enterprises. Visit the SBA site to get a complete listing of all the centers located in different states.

Office of Women's Business Ownership
www.sba.gov

SBA's Office of Women's Business Ownership (OWBO) oversees the WBC network, which provides entrepreneurs (especially women who are economically or socially disadvantaged) comprehensive training and counseling on a variety of topics in several languages.

SCORE
www.score.org

SBA SCORE
SCORE offices provides business training and education online and in person at the SBA offices. Services includes workshops on various business topics, online course and coaching with SCORE counselors.
Visit SCORE online to schedule an appointment.

Veteran's Business Outreach Centers
www.sba.gov

The **Veterans Business Outreach Program** (VBOP) is designed to provide veterans with business development assistance. The services include business training, technical coaching, mentoring, and referrals. Visit the SBA site for a complete listing and location of centers.

North American Industry Classification System (NACIS)
census.gov/eos/www/nacis

Census Bureau classifies businesses and assigns numbers based on a specific industry with the purpose to analyze and collect statistical data on the growth of U.S. businesses.

Women 2 Contract
women2contract.com

An online portal from the Women's Entrepreneurial Opportunity Project, Inc. (WEOP), containing educational information and resources related to federal contracting.

**CONTRATULATIONS!**

You have finished reading the entire contents of this book and now the rest is up to you.

**GET READY, SET AND GO** – You are off to the race to build your business with contract opportunities!

# ORGANIZATIONS SUPPORTING WOMEN

As you grow your business, seek out organizations and associations that support your business development. Organizations, such as The **Women's Entrepreneurial Opportunity Project Inc**. (WEOP) is a great example. WEOP, a non-profit organization founded in 1999, is dedicated to supporting the growth and expansion of women in business. Since inception, WEOP continues to provide a calendar of special events, specialized workshops on a range of business topics and educational classes conducted by industry professionals.

WEOP is also a membership organization for a community of like-minded entrepreneurial women. Joining as a member is a great way to connect with a network of phenomenal women making great things happen! The live events are conducted in Georgia, however, you can also join the global network online at **www.women2contract.com**.

You can learn more about the fabulous learning events, recreational outings, and networking events that WEOP has to offer at www.WEOP.org. Don't miss out on one of Atlanta's best-kept secrets. Want to stay connected, you can subscribe to get a monthly newsletter filled with great events and information to keep you informed.

Don't let anything stop you from pursuing your dreams of entrepreneurship!

**www.weop.org**

**www.women2contract.com**

404.681.2497

Made in the USA
Columbia, SC
14 January 2020